Alms and Vagabonds

Alms and Vagabonds

BUDDHIST TEMPLES AND POPULAR PATRONAGE IN MEDIEVAL JAPAN

Janet R. Goodwin

UNIVERSITY OF HAWAII PRESS

HONOLULU

© 1994 University of Hawaii Press
All rights reserved
Printed in the United States of America

94 95 96 97 98 99   5 4 3 2 1

Library of Congress Cataloging-in-Publication Data
Goodwin, Janet R., 1939–
Alms and Vagabonds: Buddhist temples and popular patronage in
medieval Japan / Janet R. Goodwin.
        p.   cm.
ISBN 0-8248-1547-5
1. Buddhist temple finance—Japan.   2. Buddhist giving.
3. Buddhism—Japan—History—1185–1600.   I. Title.
BQ5136.3.J3G66   1994
294.3'65'09520902—dc20   93-31406
                                      CIP

University of Hawaii Press books are printed on acid-free paper
and meet the guidelines for permanence and durability
of the Council on Library Resources

Designed by Paula Newcomb

Contents

MEDIEVAL JAPAN

1. Tsushima
2. Iki
KYŪSHŪ
3. Hizen
4. Chikuzen
5. Buzen
6. Chikugo
7. Bungo
8. Higo
9. Hyūga
10. Satsuma
11. Ōsumi
SHIKOKU
12. Iyo
13. Sanuki
14. Tosa
15. Awa
HONSHŪ
16. Nagato
17. Suō
18. Iwami
19. Aki
20. Izumo
21. Bingo
22. Hōki
23. Bitchū
24. Inaba
25. Mimasaka
26. Bizen
27. Tajima
28. Harima
29. Awaji
30. Tango
31. Tanba
32. Settsu
33. Izumi
34. Kawachi
35. Kii
36. Yamato
37. Wakasa
38. Yamashiro
39. Ōmi
40. Iga
41. Ise
42. Shima
43. Echizen
44. Mino
45. Owari
46. Mikawa
47. Noto
48. Kaga
49. Etchū
50. Hida
51. Shinano
52. Tōtōmi
53. Suruga
54. Kai
55. Sagami
56. Izu
57. Sado
58. Echigo
59. Kōzuke
60. Musashi
61. Dewa
62. Mutsu
63. Shimotsuke
64. Hitachi
65. Shimōsa
66. Kazusa
67. Awa

Aki (19)
Awa (Honshū) (67)
Awa (Shikoku) (15)
Awaji (29)
Bingo (21)
Bitchū (23)
Bizen (26)
Bungo (7)
Buzen (5)
Chikugo (6)
Chikuzen (4)
Dewa (61)
Echigo (58)
Echizen (43)
Etchū (49)
Harima (28)
Hida (50)
Higo (8)
Hitachi (64)
Hizen (3)
Hōki (22)
Hyūga (9)
Iga (40)
Iki (2)
Inaba (24)
Ise (41)
Iwami (18)
Iyo (12)
Izu (56)
Izumi (33)
Izumo (20)
Kaga (48)
Kai (54)
Kawachi (34)
Kazusa (66)
Kii (35)
Kōzuke (59)
Mikawa (46)
Mimasaka (25)
Mino (44)
Musashi (60)
Mutsu (62)
Nagato (16)
Noto (47)
Ōmi (39)
Ōsumi (11)
Owari (45)
Sado (57)
Sagami (55)
Sanuki (13)
Satsuma (10)
Settsu (32)
Shima (42)
Shimōsa (65)
Shimotsuke (63)
Shinano (51)
Suō (17)
Suruga (53)
Tajima (27)
Tanba (31)
Tango (30)
Tōtōmi (52)
Tosa (14)
Tsushima (1)
Wakasa (37)
Yamashiro (38)
Yamato (36)

62
61
63 64
65 66
58 59 60 67
57 55 Kamakura
54 56
51 53
47 49 52
50 45 46
48 44 42
43
39 41
Kyōto 37 40 Kasagi
30 38 ● Nara
31 32 34 36 35
27 28 33
24 25 29
22 26
23 13 15
20 Onomichi
21 14
18 19 12
17
16
5 7
4 6 9
1 3 8 11
2 10

Acknowledgments

This book would not have been possible without the help and encouragement of many teachers, friends, and colleagues. The work had its genesis during my graduate studies at the University of California at Berkeley, when Delmer Brown piqued my curiosity about Kamakura Buddhism and urged me to study the topic further. The book developed in a somewhat different direction from the dissertation that I completed under his supervision, but I remain beholden to Professor Brown for rigorous scholarly training and sympathetic support during and after my graduate years.

I am also grateful to Peter Nosco, my friend and colleague at the University of Southern California, for constant encouragement while I was writing the book and waiting for a decision on publication, for a critical reading of the manuscript, and for invaluable advice on the publication process. Others who were both keen critics and supporters were Bruce Coats, Hosea Hirata, Stanleigh Jones, Michele Marra, Lynne Miyake, Samuel Yamashita, and Eri Yasuhara. Over many a glass of beer and order of pizza, my friends and colleagues in Los Angeles helped me to evaluate the manuscript and shared with me their own research on Japanese history and literature. Britten Dean of California State University, Stanislaus, one of my earliest teachers of Asian history, provided valuable advice on one of the articles that became a chapter of this book.

I also wish to express my appreciation to the two anonymous readers for the University of Hawaii Press, for their constructive analyses of the manuscript; to Patricia Crosby, for being a congenial and encouraging editor; and to John Griswold and Jacques Vidal, for their assistance in producing the map that appears in the book. Earlier versions of some portions of this book appeared in the *Journal of Asian Studies, Monumenta Nipponica,* and the *Japanese Journal of Religious Studies* (see the bibliography for citations). I express my appreciation to the editors of these journals for permission to use this material.

I am also grateful to my parents, W. E. and Ruth Durstine, for teaching me the value of education and intellectual achievement, and for always providing me with unconditional support. My husband, Jim Goodwin, who nagged me to finish the book, labored over the map, and made sure that all necessary computers and printers were in working order, has been my best friend, my keenest critic, and my strongest supporter. It is to Jim and to my parents that this book is dedicated.

University of Aizu
Aizu-Wakamatsu, Japan

One

INTRODUCTION: THE KAMAKURA BUDDHIST TRANSFORMATION

In the year 1250 the monks of Taimyōji, a temple in the remote Kyūshū province of Ōsumi, sought the help of the Buddhist faithful to restore the temple's main worship hall. In a written appeal for donations, the monks lamented: "The roof tiles are riddled with holes and rain pours in through the ceiling. . . . The walls have crumbled, and the wind chills us." For assistance in their project, they turned to masses of lay believers, who were asked to support the temple in any small way that they could: "Even if you donate only a scrap of paper or a half-penny, this is our hope: that specks of dust will accumulate to form a mountain. Even if you donate only a small tool or a scrap of wood, this is our prayer: that dewdrops will form an ocean" (Takeuchi 1971–1991, 10:171–172 [doc. 7221]).

Like monks of many temples in Japan in the Kamakura period (1185–1333), those of Taimyōji sought help through a *kanjin* campaign, a drive for contributions from the general public. Donations were sought from all levels of society, and the Taimyōji monks' emphasis on the cumulative value of many small gifts was repeated time and time again in similar efforts by other temples. The mass appeal of such kanjin campaigns suited the spirit of outreach and evangelism that characterized Buddhism of the Kamakura age.

Kanjin campaigns became one of the vehicles by which Buddhist monks spread their teachings to the general populace. Acting as preachers as well as fundraisers, solicitors traveled highways and haunted urban marketplaces, exhorting potential donors with promises of rebirth in paradise. Donations supported temple construction, religious services, and the making of sacred images;

charity to lepers and other outcasts; and public works projects such as roads, bridges, and irrigation systems. Activities funded by kanjin campaigns made religious institutions and their teachings important factors in the lives of all Japanese. Bridges and roads not only served the public welfare, they also conveyed the idea of Buddhist compassion for all people; temples and pagodas became constant reminders of the dominance of Buddhist institutions in both religious and secular life.

Though public campaigns for donations were conducted occasionally in the Nara period (710–794) and somewhat more frequently throughout the Heian period (794–1185), they increased in frequency at the end of the eleventh century. Thereafter, kanjin campaigns became a regular means of temple fundraising, expanding in scope and obtaining recognition and assistance from state authorities. Kanjin campaigns, in short, took on new forms and public significance in the late Heian and Kamakura ages, a period generally characterized as one of transformation in Japanese Buddhism as a whole.

This phenomenon is called "Kamakura Buddhism." The term embraces a variety of developments in Buddhist institutions, teachings, and practices in the late Heian and Kamakura periods and is often used to denote a radically different religious system from its predecessors in the classical Nara and early Heian ages. In the light of recent research, which I will discuss later in this chapter, it seems unreasonable to argue for an abrupt break with the past. Yet there are significant differences in two areas: the relationship between the Buddhist system and the individual lay believer, and the interaction between Buddhist institutions and the secular community at all levels from village to nation. A study of kanjin campaigns can illuminate both areas of difference, since campaigns were one way that Buddhist institutions reached individual believers and institutions formed ties with secular communities.

I will examine the way in which the very different needs of monks and of lay supporters converged to encourage cooperation in temple building and the spread of the Buddhist word. In so doing, I will consider both the religious mission of Buddhist institutions and the economy that supported these institutions: not only were they both important factors in change, but they cannot be disentangled. This is particularly so in regard to the kanjin campaign, which used evangelistic methods to benefit temple finances and, in exchange for land, rice, or money, offered the grace of the buddhas.

Sources

For information on kanjin campaigns, I have examined sources of a variety of types and from a wide geographical area, concentrating primarily on the early medieval period, the eleventh through fourteenth centuries. Although none of these sources can be verified as individually complete and accurate, together they provide a reliable picture of kanjin campaigns.

The evidence for this study includes both documentary and literary sources. The Taimyōji monks' appeal is an example of the *kanjinjō*, a request for donations that was either circulated among potential givers or used as a script from which solicitors read appropriate passages. Although only a handful of kanjinjō are available, other sources suggest that they were issued fairly often; their content sheds light on the aims and methods of kanjin campaigns as well as on the appeals thought likely to attract donations. Records of actual donations, though even more scarce, also provide valuable information. Other evidence includes government edicts authorizing or regulating kanjin campaigns, registers of temple holdings, contemporary diaries and letters, inscriptions, and extant buildings, images, and other items funded by kanjin means.

These sources are supplemented by information from literary sources, especially *setsuwa* (tale) collections. Although setsuwa are fiction, historians often use them to illuminate the lives of provincial and urban commoners, who appear far too rarely in contemporary records. As Barbara Ruch suggests, literary sources are hardly more suspect than "factual" evidence, which can be altered or forged (1990:502); and they may in a sense be truer, simply because they had to ring true to contemporary audiences. The idealized portraits of solicitors and donors in setsuwa anecdotes illustrate what was expected of those involved in kanjin campaigns and set patterns that real solicitors and donors sometimes tried to follow; furthermore, setsuwa anecdotes themselves were often reworked to be used as kanjin appeals, and they thus have many commonalities with kanjinjō.

Kanjin campaigns were conducted all over Japan, from central regions such as the Kinai (surrounding the capital at Kyōto and the former capital at Nara) and the Inland Sea coast to remote provincial locations such as the Japan Sea coast and Ōsumi in southern Kyūshū. The aims and methods of kanjin campaigns are remarkably consistent from one locality to another, permitting broad statements about the kanjin process in Japan as a whole. The most complete and systematic evidence comes from central regions, where many temples and their landholdings were located. These were also the most economically advanced regions in Japan: they had the finest roads and ports, and they were the earliest regions to develop agricultural surpluses and markets, and to use cash as a medium of exchange. Thus it made sense for temples to concentrate their efforts on these regions, where people had the wherewithal to give and where gifts could be transported easily to the temple. There is no indication, however, that kanjin was a phenomenon of the center (that is, the central elite) that spread outward to remote locations, since provincial kanjin efforts can be traced about as far back in time as can those of the central regions.

Interpretive Questions: Anti-Structure and Muen

In pursuing this study, I have found several interpretive constructs extremely helpful. This book has been informed especially by the insights of Victor Turner and Amino Yoshihiko. Turner (1969, 1974) maintains that certain individuals, groups, places, and conditions exist outside, on the margins of, and at the very bottom of the institutionalized arrangement of positions and statuses called social structure. Turner defines these phenomena as "anti-structure," which, he argues, is characterized by a special type of community termed *communitas*, in which generic human bonds replace hierarchy and cleavage. Amino (1978b) introduces the concept of muen, which he defines as the condition of being unattached to a particular institution (except the throne), overlord (except the emperor), or place (except Japan itself). Amino's definition of Japan as a community of the whole comes close to the sense of communitas as defined by Turner, and Amino's muen individuals are close to Turner's marginals or outsiders.

The concepts of communitas and muen have important implications for a study of kanjin campaigns. To begin with, when solicitors requested "a speck of dust" or "a small tool," they were not merely valorizing tokens of faith and devotion (the equivalent of the Christian widow's mite), they were also constructing communities of donors bound by a common religious purpose (the welfare of the temple) and a common individual goal (rebirth in paradise). Membership in this collectivity depended neither on one's social or political status nor on the size of one's gift, since the smallest gift invited the supreme reward of salvation. Thus a sense of communitas was inherent in the process by which kanjin formed communities. The collectivities formed in this process opened new possibilities for cooperative action not only in temple building, but in other matters as well.

It would appear that such communities were best formed in the realm of anti-structure, since structural ties could challenge the bonds of communitas. This contention is supported by the work of Amino (1978b:49, 167; 1975:358–367), who points out the muen nature of kanjin solicitors and many of the temples involved in kanjin campaigns. He defines a muen temple as one supported not by landholding but by mendicancy and small donations. Furthermore, kanjin solicitors often referred to themselves as muen, indicating that they were not regular monks at any temple. In order to collect donations, they used locations, such as roads and ports, that were under only the throne's jurisdiction, and the rights of solicitors to operate in these venues were of the same order as the rights of peddler-craftsmen who traveled freely, licensed by the throne and under no other authority. The muen status gave kanjin solicitors the freedom to cross boundaries and transcend old structures, as I will illustrate at several points in later chapters.

The central theme of this book is the interaction between Buddhist institutions and lay society, as demonstrated by kanjin campaigns. Specifically, I will examine the ways in which kanjin campaigns contributed to the formation of collectivities in society as a whole, bringing models of community to secular life.

Subsequent chapters will take up the kanjin process in detail. Chapter 2 will discuss kanjin prior to the end of the twelfth century, exploring the role of economic change and the contribution of new economic concepts to gift seeking and giving. Chapter 3 will outline the basic aims and appeals of kanjin efforts through a case study of a campaign conducted by a small temple. Chapter 4 will provide another case study, this time of a nationwide campaign intended to fulfill a broad integrative function. Chapter 5 will examine the role of kanjin campaigns and solicitors in a wide variety of projects that enhanced local power and contributed to the solidarity of local communities. In Chapter 6, the conclusion, I will return to the issues of anti-structure and muen to assess the contributions of the kanjin process to the development of Buddhist thought and institutions and to consider its effect on some of the structures of society as a whole. Throughout the book, I will ask how people were persuaded to donate to kanjin campaigns, what rewards they were offered and what these rewards meant to them, and how the kanjin process was used both by temples and by individual lay donors for their own sometimes conflicting ends.

The Historiography of Kamakura Buddhism

Kamakura Buddhism involved changes on two levels, that of the individual believer and that of the Buddhist institution. As far as the individual was concerned, the fundamental element of Kamakura Buddhism was the inclusion—in an actual, not a theoretical, sense—of all individuals in the category of those considered eligible for salvation. In terms of institutional developments, Buddhism's base of support expanded rapidly, stimulated by social and economic change in the late Heian and Kamakura periods. The phenomenon involved all elements of Buddhist society: established temples and their monks, innovative teachers who broke away from established Buddhism and founded independent sects, and isolated hermits, ascetics, and preachers. Both the new sects and outreach movements within the established schools emphasized faith and simple practice for the lay believer, and the spiritual welfare of the individual became an overwhelming concern. Within the monasteries, reform movements emphasizing purity and sincerity challenged the tendency for clergy to accumulate wealth and political power at the expense of their religious mission. Although strictly speaking these monastic movements involved only the clergy, they forced monks to rethink their relationship to lay believers and led, in many cases, to active efforts at evangelism and charity.

Kanjin campaigns, evangelistic in nature and sometimes conducted for charitable purposes, played a significant part in these movements and became one vehicle of change in Kamakura Buddhism. Yet campaigns were held almost exclusively by temples of existing schools, often characterized as the elitist establishment against which new movements reacted. Thus the matter of kanjin raises fundamental questions: how existing schools participated in the change and, ultimately, how and why the change occurred.

This final question has long been a subject for debate, and the debate itself is of considerable historiographical interest. Standard accounts that prevailed until the mid-1970s (and continue to inform textbooks) attributed the Kamakura transformation entirely to new sects that broke both doctrinally and organizationally with established institutions. The central change in Kamakura, according to this argument, was the introduction of Buddhism to the people by the Pure Land masters Hōnen (1133-1212) and Shinran (1173-1262), and the Lotus school founder Nichiren (1222-1282). Rinzai and Sōtō, the two branches of Zen that were established in the Kamakura period, were not designed for the common folk, but they contributed to the expansion of Buddhism through their appeal to provincial warriors. Less attention is paid to the itinerant Pure Land master Ippen (1239-1289), who actively proselytized among the people but maintained his devotion to established temples and practices. The existing *kenmitsu* schools—the Nara schools, established in the seventh and eighth centuries in the old capital of Nara, and Tendai and Shingon, the dominant schools of the Heian period—are portrayed as corrupt and moribund, their influence rapidly waning, their reform efforts ultimately fruitless.[1]

The new Buddhism of the Kamakura age, according to this view, was purged of the excessive rituals and emphasis on material splendor that had made its Heian counterpart a rich person's religion. Instead, people flocked to the pietistic sects, following either the Pure Land admonition to rely on the compassionate Buddha Amida and to recite his praises in a formula termed the *nenbutsu* or the admonition to recite the Lotus sūtra title as instructed by Nichiren. The fact that the pietistic sects grew rapidly in the late medieval age lent credence to the standard argument, which was attractive for other reasons as well: the founders of the new sects were charismatic individuals who gave life to history, and their direct, simple teachings invited comparison with the Protestant Reformation. Thus the story of Kamakura Buddhism became a dramatic tale of pious founders battling a stagnant, corrupt ortho-doxy to purify Buddhism and broaden its teachings to embrace all men and women.

That view by now has been rejected as overly simplistic. Just as some historians have questioned the abruptness and complete-ness of the transfer of political power from aristocrat to warrior, others have asked whether religious change occurred so quickly, so unambiguously, and in a way so neatly explained. The challenge comes from two directions: from studies of Buddhist institutions and their relationship to secular society, and from studies of the beliefs and practices of ordinary people.[2] More than one scholar has argued that it was the kenmitsu institutions and their clergy that occupied the religious mainstream of the Kamakura age and that in their own time the sectarian movements, so important later, were not very influential (e.g., Kuroda 1980:iii; Taira 1984:290; Morrell 1985:9–10). These findings suggest, moreover, that Kamakura Buddhism was eclectic, embracing old as well as new teachings, that sectarian boundaries were not always strictly drawn, and that the vigor of new teachings permeated the ken-mitsu schools as well as the newly established sects.

The very terminology used to distinguish the sectarian move-ments from established institutions presents a distorted picture of Kamakura Buddhism. The Pure Land, Lotus, and Zen sects are grouped together under the rubric "new Buddhism," in contrast to the term "old Buddhism," which paints the kenmitsu schools with the dismal colors of reaction. In addition, the term "new" makes the sectarian movements seem more revolutionary than they really were. In many ways they continued and refined inno-vative practices that had their origin in the kenmitsu schools: sec-tarian practices such as the nenbutsu, reverence for the Lotus sūtra, and Zen meditation had penetrated kenmitsu Buddhism, especially Tendai, well before the Kamakura period. Moreover, when the kenmitsu schools broadened their evangelical efforts, they used some of the same devices adopted by Pure Land and Lotus masters to reach out to the common people.

According to James H. Foard, "The worst damage wrought by the notion that Kamakura Buddhism consisted of five sects is that it has separated the similar and lumped together the dissimi-lar" (1980:266). Foard criticizes the standard explanation for neglecting movements that contributed to the Kamakura transformation, such as devotional cults and mendicant orders within the kenmitsu schools. In Foard's view, to which I also subscribe, the Kamakura transformation must be attributed to all agents of change, whether they broke away from existing institutions or created evangelical movements within these institutions. In short, both kenmitsu schools and new sects contributed to the "central religious change of the Kamakura period," which, according to Foard, "resulted from a new affirmation: that an individual of any social or ecclesiastical standing could immediately reap the full benefits of Buddhist salvation, or such lesser benefits as health and prosperity, through some form of direct, personal devotion to a particular Buddha, bodhisattva, sūtra or saint" (1980:267). Seen in this way, the salient features of Kamakura Buddhism are devotionalism and an emphasis on the salvation of the individual, which were concerns of both the kenmitsu schools and the new sects.

Nonetheless there was a major distinction between the kenmitsu schools and the new movements: the organizational and doctrinal exclusivity that allows us unambiguously to use the term "sects" for the latter. The sects not only made an institutional break with kenmitsu Buddhism, they expected wholehearted and exclusive devotion from their clerics and lay followers. Furthermore, while kenmitsu teachings embraced a plurality of beliefs and practices, the sects each chose a single practice and denied the value of others.

On closer view, however, even this distinction begins to evaporate. Rinzai Zen was eclectic and tolerant in its early days, and Eisai, the man generally credited with bringing it to Japan, also served the kenmitsu temple Tōdaiji as the head of its kanjin office. Hōnen's practice of esoteric rituals contradicted his emphasis on the nenbutsu as the sole avenue to salvation (Matsunaga and Matsunaga 1974–1976, 2:61). Shinran did not think of himself as the founder of an independent sect; the formation of "sectarian identity" within Shinran's Jōdo Shinshū can be seen as an evolutionary process that only began with Shinran's formative vision (Dobbins 1986:331). Moreover, the sects eventually built temples and installed images in them, organized their clergy into hierarchies, conducted funerals, and collected donations from their faithful lay believers—practices that made them resemble the kenmitsu schools. In fact, until they adopted some of these practices, the influence of the sects was limited, indicating that the popularization attributed to them came in part from their role in spreading practices that their founders had originally rejected. Thus even hindsight cannot diminish the continued importance of the kenmitsu schools, both in their own time and as an influence on later religious developments.

Although contemporary scholars are now paying the necessary attention to the kenmitsu schools and changes within them, very little work has been done on the relationship between the Kamakura transformation and socioeconomic change. While the focus was still exclusively on the new sects, it was often said that the decline of aristocratic society and the rise of the warrior class encouraged the development of new religious teachings and modes of organization suited to warriors' and commoners' needs. This proposition, however, was not explored in any detail, perhaps because it seemed so obvious. But if some agents of religious change worked within the kenmitsu schools, whose extensive landholdings made them part of the aristocratic establishment, then the link between religious and socioeconomic change becomes more complex. Thus it should be useful to examine in detail such phenomena as economic growth, the diffusion of political power, and the search for religious validation by power holders and power seekers. In other words, it is necessary to consider not only the ideas that informed Kamakura Buddhism, but also the way in which those ideas interacted with formal institutions and informal social structures.[3]

The central impulse of Kamakura Buddhism, outreach to the lay community, required a search for converts, often synonymous with a search for patrons. Thus kanjin campaigns, the chief means by which kenmitsu temples sought the support of masses of lay believers, concern not only temple economics but also the spread of Buddhist teachings through evangelism and the connection of that process with historical change in society as a whole. An examination of kanjin campaigns should contribute to a thorough and accurate picture of Kamakura Buddhism that recognizes the continued importance of the kenmitsu schools in religious, political, and economic terms, and considers commonalities among all Buddhist schools—their shared religious base and practices, both old and new, and their similar reactions to religious and secular stimuli.

Patronage and Temple Economics

Even before the Kamakura transformation, Buddhism was accessible in theory to all men and women. The teaching that everyone had a buddha-nature and thus could eventually attain buddhahood had strong scriptural support, especially in the Lotus sūtra, the central text of the powerful Tendai school. Prior to the twelfth century, however, established Buddhist institutions concentrated on serving the needs of the state and its central aristocracy rather than those of the people. Important temples received almost all their support from aristocratic families and the state. Their clergy, in turn, focused their efforts on aiding their supporters. An ailing ruler, a princess about to give birth, a province in need of rain to produce tax rice: these were typically the intended beneficiaries of the clergy's prayers. In the Nara period, when heterodox preachers and magicoreligious practitioners tried to spread Buddhism among the people, they were suppressed by the government, which feared the potential for disruption inherent in popular religious movements.

Despite the efforts of the government, the word did get to the people, at least on a limited basis. We have little documentary information in this regard, but the ninth-century setsuwa collection *Nihon ryōiki* depicts popular evangelists and lay believers who promoted Buddhism by constructing village chapels. Despite this evidence, it is difficult to argue that important Buddhist temples routinely viewed ordinary people as targets for evangelism or that the masses flocked to temples. Commoners, especially those considered rude and dirty, were probably not welcome at institutions that catered to the aristocracy, and we can imagine that ordinary folk were intimidated by the common perception that buddhahood depended on one's ability to undergo rigorous practices, study abstruse texts, or donate large sums to temples. Temples, moreover, were part of the elite political system that monopolized farmland and taxed and worked the peasant population. It seems likely that peasants viewed Buddhist institutions as rulers and landlords rather than as sources of comfort and salvation.

If important kenmitsu temples paid little attention to ordinary people until the late Heian period, it was partly because monks were busy scrambling for patrons. Their religious mission required temples to construct buildings, make images, and feed and clothe the monks whose prayers were thought to benefit society. These were activities that had to be supported by the lay community—in particular by those who had wealth and power. In seeking the support of high-placed patrons, monks became land managers and politicians; when political and economic circumstances made it advantageous to seek support from a broader social base, monks from the same temples became leaders of kanjin campaigns. In other words, the dual nature of temples as religious and economic institutions colored their interactions with the public.

Temples depended on a complex system of patronage. In the Nara and early Heian periods, private sponsorship by noble families supplemented government funding in the form of "sustenance households" of peasants, whose produce was earmarked for particular temples. By the late Heian period, however, most large temples had come to depend on the *shōen* (estate) system that supported almost all propertied institutions of the time.

Shōen were agricultural holdings that were not owned outright by any single party. Instead, a hierarchy of individuals or institutions had legal rights to the produce of the land as well as designated management rights and obligations. For the most part temples held shōen as absentee proprietors, leaving the day-to-day management of affairs to on-site managers. The proprietor's main task was to lobby the government for tax exemptions and protection against provincial officials and the officers of neighboring shōen, either of whom might trespass a shōen's borders and confiscate its crops.

Crucial to temple welfare was the ability to obtain such exemptions and protection as well as commendations of new fields. In this highly competitive process, temples with close connections to the imperial family and the aristocracy had a considerable edge. For example, landholding in Yamato province was dominated by Kōfukuji, family temple of the powerful Fujiwara, and Tōdaiji, established as a national temple by the eighth-century emperor Shōmu, had numerous holdings throughout western Japan. The Shingon establishment at Mt. Kōya and the Tendai establishment at Mt. Hiei, both strongly supported by important figures at court, had significant holdings in their home provinces and elsewhere. Other temples, including some of venerable age and distinguished origin, fell behind in the fray. Small temples and newly established ones were not competitive: there was just not enough land to go around. Unsuccessful efforts to obtain or augment landholdings put some temples in a perpetual state of crisis. In the late Heian period, even powerful temples found that they could no longer rely entirely on shōen proprietorships for their support, and this problem intensified in the Kamakura age. This is one reason that temples turned increasingly to kanjin campaigns to supplement their income. It was not that the shōen system was declining, as has sometimes been suggested; rather, it was changing to the detriment of absentee proprietors and to the advantage of local managers and prosperous cultivators. Local magnates sponsored small-scale land reclamation projects that increased the productivity of their holdings (Inagaki 1975:168–182), no doubt keeping some of the profits for themselves. When a warrior government (the *bakufu*) was installed in Kamakura in the late twelfth century, its representatives—military stewards called *jitō*—were placed on many shōen and given a share of their income, and they too maximized their own profits, sometimes refusing to forward the proprietor's share of income from the fields. While some temples suffered, others discovered a new opportunity: to tap the time, wealth, and religious potential of a new class of people produced by political and economic change. One way to do so was through the kanjin campaign.

This development was also encouraged by an extramonastic movement that began in the second half of the Heian period, similar to the one suppressed in the Nara period but much larger in scope. Inoue Mitsusada suggests that by the tenth century state control over religious activity had begun to unravel, and rules governing proselytization could be safely ignored (1956:219). In addition, perhaps because they spent so much effort competing for shōen rights and currying favor with the aristocracy, large kenmitsu temples were widely perceived as corrupt. This perception, along with economic growth at lower levels of society, contributed to a new religious spirit that encouraged Buddhist practice outside monastery walls—in other words, by muen individuals. Hermits, ascetics, and popular preachers called *hijiri*—saints or holy persons—spread simplified Buddhist teachings among the people. Hijiri found fertile ground in newly prosperous folk, but their teachings appealed to the poor and simple as well. By weaving Buddhist elements into the magicoreligious folk beliefs that dominated rural religious life, Heian period hijiri prepared the way for the significant changes in Buddhism of the Kamakura age. Moreover, it was muen hijiri who collected donations to kanjin campaigns, which then became a common source of funding for both small temples with scant access to public funds or noble patrons and large temples that needed to supplement income from agricultural land. The second half of the Heian period saw an explosion of popular evangelism on the part of hijiri acting outside formal institutions; these activities, ironically, sometimes benefited the very temples where hijiri had declined to practice. Moreover, the implicit criticism by hijiri caused regular monks to reconsider the relationship of their own institutions to the lay public, thus preparing these institutions to expand their base of support.

Mappō *and the Nara Revival*

The attempt to reach a new class of supporters was also shaped by a Buddhist theory of time and history that seemed to dictate the opening of Buddhism to all potential believers. Although the new religious enthusiasts of the late Heian and Kamakura periods did not necessarily accept this theory in all its implications, they turned to Buddhism for reasons of their own, in which the desire for salvation was entwined with the need to validate their own family structures and social positions.

The theory that dominated Buddhism of the late Heian and Kamakura periods maintained that history proceeds in cycles called *kalpas,* each one beginning with a golden age at the birth of a buddha. According to this theory, which is outlined in the scriptures, a buddha's death is followed by gradual decline until a degenerate age called mappō (the end of the law) is reached. It was thought that in mappō, a time of famine, pestilence, poverty, shortened life spans, and general despair, human beings would completely lose the ability to practice the Buddhist law. As is well known, Hōnen, Shinran, and Nichiren seized on this theory to justify their advocacy of simple religious practice; but mappō thought influenced many other religious developments in the late Heian and Kamakura age, sometimes in rather subtle ways.

It is important to remember that the kalpa theory was not a theory of linear decay, but rather one of cyclical decline and renewal. Thus mappō would be followed by a gradual improvement in both religious and material conditions until the birth of a new buddha and a renewal of the golden age. Unlike theories of the Christian apocalypse, the "messiah" was to come in a fortunate era, not in the time of deepest misery. Both the age of despair and that of regeneration caught the imagination of medieval Japanese. The onset of mappō had been calculated as 1052,[4] and in the view of pious monks, pomp and corruption at their own monasteries seemed to point to decline. This apparent degeneration inspired many Buddhist thinkers, in the kenmitsu schools as well as in the pietistic sects, to consider methods of dealing with the hazards of a degenerate age. According to some views, the times made all men and women equal in their spiritual poverty; there was thus no reason, if there had ever been one, to deny a chance for salvation to those who lacked knowledge or virtue. In other views the desperate need to preserve the Buddhist law required the cooperation of all potential believers. As a result, both the kenmitsu schools and the pietistic sects expounded their teachings broadly, with little regard for their listeners' social standing or level of virtue. Thus religious impulse joined with economic need and opportunity to impel the spread of Buddhist teachings to all people.

Kalpa theory suggested various approaches to personal virtue and religious practice on the part of monks themselves. Some, like Hōnen and Shinran, recommended faith and emphasized the uselessness of personal effort, while others insisted that the degeneracy of the times demanded vigorous personal effort to follow the Buddhist law. Within the kenmitsu temples, especially those located in Nara, monks sought to revive their schools in the days of mappō by returning to the purity of the time of Shakyamuni, the historical Buddha (Yoshida 1972:167). At the core of this movement, called the Nara revival, lay a renewed emphasis on the precepts, an attempt to reach out to lay believers through evangelism and charity, and a concern with the preservation and restoration of Buddhism's physical framework of images and temples. The thread connecting these aims was the desire to build a community of monks and lay believers. Leading figures of the Nara revival included Chōgen (1121–1206), Jōkei (1155–1212), and Eizon (1201–1290), each a leader of kanjin campaigns to restore his temple (and a subject of subsequent chapters of this book).

Jōkei and Eizon were known for their diligent efforts to keep the monastic precepts and to persuade their fellow monks to do likewise. As a result of their and others' teachings, a core of "Ritsu" (precept keeping) monks developed within many of the Nara temples. Their strict lives distinguished them from the general monastic population, who preferred a looser approach to the minute regulations on daily conduct, especially the prohibition against amassing private wealth. The attempt to restore the precepts has been seen as a purely monastic movement (Foard 1980:266); yet Ritsu monks engaged in the very activities that directly touched lay believers, such as kanjin campaigns, charity, public building projects, and funeral services. These activities represented a second dimension to their religious practice: the urge to help all beings, at whatever stage of progress toward enlightenment. Implicit in the emphasis on the precepts was the value set on personal virtue for those who would save others.

This emphasis, moreover, was a complex reaction to mappō thought and to kalpa theory in general. One motivation for keeping the precepts was the consciousness that only purity and goodness could ward off the degeneracy of the current age. But the attempt to return to the purity of Shakyamuni's time indicates a sense of optimism that it was possible to accomplish such a task. Leading figures of the Nara revival such as Jōkei, moreover, set their sights on the upswing of the kalpa rather than on mappō, focusing on Miroku, the Buddha of the future, who was expected to appear on earth at kalpa's end and repeat Shakyamuni's mission. Restorers of the Nara schools had one eye on the degenerate present but the other on a golden future equated with a golden past.

The expectation of Miroku's advent was one general conclusion of the kalpa theory. The fear of mappō combined with the anticipation of a utopian future generated a desire to preserve the good things of the present—Buddhist texts, images, and temples —through dark times until the advent of the new Buddha. "Until Miroku's coming" became a rallying cry for preservation efforts of all kinds, including the burial of sūtras for safekeeping and the use of durable stone for sacred images. For example, early in the thirteenth century the Kōfukuji abbot Gaen commissioned an engraving of Miroku on a cliff facing the small temple Ōnodera in Yamato province. Kōfukuji's account of the dedication ceremony explains the choice of material: "Even though their appearances are splendid, wooden images and paintings—alas—cannot help but decay. But when it comes to stone images, they can just about last until the advent of Miroku in the distant future" (*Kōfukuji bettō shidai* 1917:29).

Generally speaking, the Nara revival was marked by an emphasis on preservation and restoration, which inspired efforts to establish new temples and rebuild old ones that had fallen into decay. When warriors burned the great Nara temple Tōdaiji to the ground in 1180, the temple's reconstruction, headed by the kanjin hijiri Chōgen, became the centerpiece of the Nara revival. The effort demanded creativity, innovation, and the cooperation of all classes of people, and it served as a model for kanjin campaigns throughout the entire nation. Campaigns such as these, which promised salvation in return for small gifts, became important vehicles for the expansion of Buddhist teachings to the general populace.

Other vehicles for disseminating Buddhist teachings among the populace were charity, public works projects, and funerals and cremations. Many of these activities were promoted by kanjin solicitors, and some were funded by donations from the public. Nara monks such as Eizon dispensed food to the outcast *hinin* and preached to them as well, urging them to adopt the bodhisattva precepts, which charged people to avoid evil, to practice virtue, and to help others. Charity and secular public works projects ingratiated monks with local leaders, helping them to establish footholds for their temples in the local community. Ritsu monks, in particular, used the rites of death to spread Buddhism among the people: common graveyards were established at Ritsu temples, Ritsu monks managed funeral services, and lower-class Ritsu affiliates cremated the dead (Hosokawa 1987:1–30). It can be argued that Ritsu monks who introduced Buddhist funeral services to the poor played as significant a part in bringing Buddhism to the masses as did leaders of the pietistic sects.

Whatever their differences, both the founders of new sects and the Nara revivalist monks responded creatively to the challenge posed by kalpa theory and the belief that the world had entered the age of mappō. Although the mappō question was of great concern to almost all the Buddhist clergy, they did not react in a uniform way, and those (such as Jōkei) who considered the progression of the entire kalpa came to somewhat different conclusions from those (such as Hōnen) who focused on mappō alone. However, motives for and methods of evangelizing lay believers were often remarkably similar, based as they were on the foundation laid by hijiri in the late Heian period. Although the sects and the kenmitsu schools might differ over the question of eclecticism, both offered lay believers easy routes to and concrete visions of salvation.

How did lay believers view the question of mappō? The standard view of the Kamakura faithful shows a despairing populace that accepted the notion of decline and turned to religion as the last hope in an age so chaotic that it seemed to validate the dire predictions in the sūtras. But there is little evidence that the lay population as a whole regarded the age with a sense of despair. True enough, conditions were difficult and people often suffered. The transition from the Heian to the Kamakura period was marked by banditry, famine, and civil war; provincial warriors grew strong while civilian aristocrats began to lose their monopoly on wealth and power. Among the laity, it was the aristocrats—the shōen proprietor class—who most feared the dangers of mappō. Few envisioned the eventual eclipse of aristocratic government by a warrior elite, yet many were aware that times were changing to their disadvantage. For them, the end of the Buddhist law mirrored their own perceptions of decline.

The new Buddhist enthusiasts of the Kamakura period, however, were not aristocrats but provincial warriors, local magnates, and small landholders. Some of them, who had begun to manipulate the shōen system to their own advantage, had little reason for despair but much for optimism. Furthermore, they needed to validate their activities in religious terms. Much of their religious energy was devoted to obtaining salvation for dead parents and other forebears, a purpose that led them to donate to temples in the name of the dead as well as to conduct memorial services and erect memorial stupas and tablets. These actions indicate an emphasis on lineage, important in justifying claims to property and achieving distinction in the local community. In addition, warriors among the faithful needed to mitigate the violence in their own and their forebears' lives; thus efforts were made to bring Buddhist salvation to those who had taken human life and to soothe the spirits of battle victims. The efforts to save the dead, based on the principle that the fruits of one's own good deeds could be passed on to chosen others, manifested the empowerment of believers rather than their helplessness.

As local economies flourished under the control of local elites, temples used kanjin campaigns to form ties with communities and their leaders. Kanjin solicitors promised donors salvation, couched in terms that reinforced the communal value of adding one's own small effort to a common cause. In exchange for alms, solicitors peddled their organizational skills, their technical expertise, and their charisma, implementing projects that benefited both the religious and the secular communities. In a later chapter I will explore the efforts of one medieval ruler to reinforce and legitimize his power through the restoration of Tōdaiji. What was true of rulers was also true of local magnates: the establishment or restoration of a local temple enhanced their prestige and their power. Moreover, when kanjin solicitors who built temples also built bridges and irrigation ponds, the benefits of these projects to society were often described in religious terms. These activities extended the power of temples, which tightened their grip on land-holdings and formed cooperative relationships with the very local figures who had threatened their rights as shōen proprietors. All this suggests that hope and ambition, rather than despair, motivated many lay men and women to form attachments with Buddhist temples.

The new associations between Buddhist institutions, on the one hand, and individuals and communities, on the other, depended much on the creation of common ground by two parties, the lay public and religious leaders, whose needs differed widely yet converged in significant ways. These needs were manifested in the methods and the goals of kanjin campaigns. Even venal methods—donations, though in theory voluntary, were sometimes assessed as taxes or as tolls—became the means to an ultimately religious end: the preservation and promotion of the Buddhist law throughout the entire kalpa, from the degenerate times of mappō to Miroku's golden future.

In this chapter I have suggested that the dynamics of change in early medieval Buddhism involved complex interactions between temples and patrons, proselytizers and proselytized, and social structure and its margins that cannot be examined outside a general context of socioeconomic change. Though a study of kanjin campaigns cannot explain all these dynamics, it can contribute to an understanding of them, especially of the roles of such seemingly disparate individuals as muen hijiri, Ritsu monks, and lay believers on every social level. The next chapter will examine the way in which socioeconomic change contributed to the early development of kanjin campaigns and suggest some of the ways that temples and lay patrons made use of one another in the process.

Before Kamakura:
Early Kanjin Campaigns

In the late Heian and Kamakura periods, socioeconomic change and the evangelistic impulse based on mappō thought impelled many temples to seek support from the public through kanjin campaigns. The practice of kanjin, however, developed long before, even before the term itself came into use. With a few exceptions, early fundraising efforts were conducted with limited aims and in limited geographical areas, but these early efforts helped to create models for later, far more extensive campaigns. When economic growth in the late Heian period placed surplus wealth in the hands of potential donors, temples began to find kanjin campaigns effective means to finance even major projects.

The expanded use of kanjin campaigns involved a process of regularization on the part of both temples and lay authorities. Most early campaigns were ad hoc ventures initiated and conducted by muen hijiri—in other words, they were phenomena of anti-structure. But as Victor Turner has pointed out, anti-structure is generally a temporary phenomenon that tends toward structure (1974:248-249); in the case of kanjin, temples seem to have made a conscious effort to bring campaigns and muen hijiri under their own control. In addition, campaigns of any substance were feasible only if they were recognized, at least implicitly, by the state. Political authorities had their own reasons for supporting temple fundraising. In the eighth century, the throne used a public campaign for temple construction to buttress its political authority, but this was an isolated instance. In the late Heian period, however, secular powers on both a national and a local scale began systematically to appropriate kanjin as a means of legitimation.

21

In short, both temples and lay authorities had reason to bring kanjin efforts under firm control. Still, the muen nature of kanjin hijiri gave them certain advantages as fundraisers, allowing them to travel freely and to appeal to all classes of people. Thus the kanjin process was never entirely subsumed under state authority or incorporated into temple structures, and muen hijiri continued to play an important part in campaigns, sometimes even to the point of clashing with a temple's regular monks.

This chapter will take up the process by which kanjin campaigns were initiated and then regularized prior to the Kamakura period, with special attention to two factors: the changing role of muen hijiri and the influence of economic change.

The Earliest Kanjin Campaigns

Sometime in the mid-Heian period, the term *kanjin* was first used to signify efforts by temples to canvass the public for contributions. That usage expanded upon the word's original meaning, the encouragement of Buddhist faith and virtue: contributing to temples was one of the good deeds that the Buddhist lay faithful were expected to perform. In original Indian Buddhism, in fact, giving alms to monks was the only act recommended to the lay believer, who could not hope to reach buddhahood through the study, ritual, and asceticism that monks practiced. The faithful believer's best chance at buddhahood was to earn enough merit through supporting monks to allow rebirth in his or her next life as a human male inclined to become a monk himself. Although Japanese Buddhists, influenced by the devotionalism of Mahayana teachings, would not have defined the role of the lay believer quite so strictly, the giving of alms was seen as a significant path toward individual salvation.

Active efforts to secure donations from lay believers and to pool these donations for a specific project began in the first centuries of Buddhism in Japan. Evidence that monks collected donations for the copying of sūtras can be found as early as 685 (Horiike 1976:5–6). Large-scale campaigns for gifts, however—at least those that reached the commoner public—were discouraged by legal restrictions on Buddhist evangelism, such as the *sōniryō* (rules for monks and nuns) in the eighth-century law codes, which regulated the daily lives of the clergy. Among other things, the regulations forbade monks and nuns to foment political dissent, to establish centers for preaching "false doctrines" to the people, and to heal illness through sorcery. Monks and nuns were allowed to beg for food only, and only for the purpose of ascetic training. Moreover, they were forbidden "to entrust the scriptures or images of Buddha to lay persons and let them visit the houses of the faithful for purposes of solicitation" (Kitagawa 1969:258–259).[1] Thus private alms collecting was categorized as illegal and unorthodox Buddhist practice. Whether the regulations addressed existing problems or only anticipated them, the government was clearly threatened by the prospect that charismatic religious figures might provoke disorder.

Not everyone obeyed the law, however, and a number of renegade "clergy"—many not officially ordained—continued to populate the religious scene of eighth-century Japan. The construction of an official system of temples in mid-century can be seen as an attempt to control this potentially dangerous situation as well as to mobilize the symbolic and ritual power of Buddhism in support of the state. The centerpiece of the project was Tōdaiji, a great temple built in the capital in an effort to legitimize and strengthen the Japanese throne. Construction was financed in part by a campaign to obtain donations from the public, a method that was probably intended to deflect protest by inviting broad participation in the project. If alms campaigns conducted privately were a threat to public authority, the solution was to bring them under public control. In so doing, the government not only appropriated the alms-collection method, but also the era's most popular and potentially dangerous evangelist.

The man chosen to head the campaign was a monk named Gyōki (668–749), at first glance a curious choice. Gyōki was one of the renegade monks who had aroused the anxiety of the state not many years before. According to a complaint registered in the fourth month of 717 in the *Shoku nihongi:*

These days the worthless monk Gyōki and his disciples swarm along the public thoroughfares, recklessly explaining ill omens, forming factions, burning their fingers [to use them as torches] and stripping skin from their elbows [on which to copy passages from the sūtras]. They go from door to door spreading false teachings and extorting donations. Claiming to be saints, they deceive the householders. Lay believers and clergy are confused, and all classes of people abandon their labor. (Aoki et al. 1989–1990, 2:26–27)

The passage suggests that Gyōki used extortionate tricks to bewitch the populace and fomented dissent against the government. In particular, he was charged with "recklessly explaining ill omens"—in other words, suggesting that disasters such as floods or famines were indications of government wrongdoing. Peasants burdened with heavy taxes may have been all too eager to blame the government for these ills as well. It was perhaps this dangerous situation that impelled the government to curry favor with Gyōki instead of suppressing him, and in 721 he was invited by Empress Genshō to lecture at court (Matsunaga and Matsunaga 1974–1976, 1:119). Shōmu (r. 724–749), her successor, granted Gyōki the official clerical title *daisōjō*, thus recognizing him as part of the Buddhist establishment, and asked for his help in building Tōdaiji. Specifically, he was asked to collect donations for the construction project.

In inviting Gyōki's participation and stressing the voluntary nature of the subscription campaign, Shōmu rejected the option of financing the project through taxes alone, which might have aroused popular protest (led, perhaps, by Gyōki himself). Perhaps the emperor believed that he could defuse objections to the expense of the grand project with the help of someone close to the people and with at least the appearance that the project had public and voluntary support. Or, as Joan R. Piggott suggests, he may have embraced Gyōki's Mahayana ideal of evangelizing all humankind (1987:123). In either case, it appears that the choice of both the method to finance the temple and the man to implement that method fit one of Shōmu's purposes in launching the project in the first place: to transcend internal conflict through claiming sacred legitimation (see Piggott 1987:5).

Thus Shōmu chose to add one more element to the complex ideology supporting the Japanese throne. Its legitimacy came, first of all, from the claim that the monarch was descended from Amaterasu, *kami* (deity) of the sun and the highest figure in the native pantheon. During the process of the centralization of power in the seventh and eighth centuries, the monarch was also promoted as a Chinese-style political ruler in charge of land and official appointments, as a Confucian ruler who nurtured his people, and as a link between cosmos and people, nature and nation, also in Chinese style. Buddhism served several important functions in the legitimizing process. Because Buddhism had come from China, it helped to reflect Chinese glory—and the idea of a powerful Chinese-style monarch—upon the Japanese political situation. Buddhist deities were asked to protect the personal welfare of the monarch and his ministers and the security and prosperity of the nation as a whole. Through patronage of temples, the monarch could demonstrate the largesse and grandeur of the throne. Devotion to Buddhism enhanced the image of the monarch as a virtuous ruler. Perhaps the most important factor, however, was that Buddhism—if its institutions and symbol system were monopolized as Shōmu intended—could help to unify Japanese society under the throne.

When Shōmu constructed an integrated system of state Buddhism with Tōdaiji at its center, he was attempting to create two concentric systems, one religious and the other political. In the first, Tōdaiji occupied the center of a radiating system, with provincial temples *(kokubunji)* on the outer ring. Tōdaiji's centrality was further symbolized by its main object of worship, a gigantic image (Daibutsu) of Roshana Buddha, from whom all phenomena were said to emanate. The political scheme placed the throne at the center of a similarly radiating system and provincial and local governments on the outer rings. Shōmu's adoption of "Roshana" as his religious name at the image's dedication ceremony (Matsunaga and Matsunaga 1974–1976, 1:121) confirms that he saw his own position as analogous to that of the Daibutsu.

Shōmu's choice of a public campaign to help finance the casting of the image supported his aim of integrating the nation with the throne at the center. His choice of Gyōki to head the campaign should also be seen in that light. In his proclamation of 743 authorizing the project, Shōmu declared, "If there are those whose hearts are moved to donate even a twig, a blade of grass, or a clump of earth to help in the construction of this image, these offerings should all be accepted. The provincial and district officials must not intrude on the people for the sake of this project and forcibly exact donations from them" (Aoki et al. 1989–1990, 2:432–433 [743/10/15]). The edict, in short, stipulated the collection of donations of any size, but only if they were voluntary. In a few days Gyōki and his followers were dispatched to gather contributions (Aoki et al. 1989–1990, 2:432–433 [743/10/19]). We have no way of knowing how successful Gyōki's campaign was or what percentage of the expense of the image was, in fact, met by voluntary donations. According to *Tōdaiji yōroku*, compiled in the early twelfth century, more than two million donors contributed rice, wood, metal, and labor to the project (1907:37, quoted in Piggott 1987:128). The truth of this account is inconsequential. The important factors are the participation of a popular leader and his ability to defuse public dissatisfaction, making the construction of Tōdaiji a national effort. Thus the great temple symbolized not only the glory of a particular emperor, but also the link between the emperor and his people, who were described as willing parties in the temple's founding.

The construction of Tōdaiji was an extraordinary project, duplicated only in the late twelfth century when that temple, burned to the ground, was restored through a national effort. In the Nara period, large temples rarely relied on public donations for construction and major repairs, though there are records of at least one other eighth-century campaign. In 781 the *shami* (novice monk) Hōkyō asked *dōzoku chishiki* (clergy and lay believers) in Ise, Mino, Owari, and Shima provinces for gifts to support the construction of a lecture hall and a bath for the monks at the temple affiliated with Tado shrine (Takeuchi 1963–1976, 1:11–12 [doc. 20]). Though we know little about this campaign, the fact that it crossed provincial boundaries suggests that it was officially sanctioned and that it may have been quite significant in terms of the people reached and the donations collected.

As for village temples, they were probably built and adorned by the people themselves. One episode in the ninth-century tale collection *Nihon ryōiki* tells of a wealthy man from Ōmi province who had vowed to copy the *Yugaron* but had been unable to do so (Kyōkai 1984:227–228; Nakamura 1973:231–233 [book 3, no. 8]). Eventually he lost his wealth and abandoned his family to become a vagabond ascetic, still keeping his vow in mind. One day he saw a vision of Miroku appearing in a bush in the precincts of a mountain temple. When local people heard of the vision, they came to see it too, bringing bags of rice, money, and clothing as donations. With these donations, the man from Ōmi was able to pay scribes to copy one hundred scrolls of the sacred text. Another tale recalls the efforts of Shingyō, a man from a powerful family in Kii province (Kyōkai 1984:247–249; Nakamura 1973:244–245 [book 3, no. 17]). Shingyō adopted the religious life, taking vows privately, and took up residence at a village temple. One night he heard groans of pain from two unfinished Buddhist images. He and a visiting monk from the Nara temple Gangōji organized a lay association to finance completion of the sculpture. The frequent mention of chishiki (believers) and village temples in these and other *Ryōiki* tales suggests that kanjin efforts may have actually been common in the eighth and ninth centuries (see Sasaki 1987:22–34), though few were conducted on a significant enough scale to warrant inclusion in contemporary records.

Hijiri: The Legmen of Kanjin Campaigns

Much of the actual work of collecting donations was performed by kanjin hijiri, sometimes also called kanjin *shami* or kanjin *sō* (monk). The term was not used very precisely; rather, it was one of several descriptive terms applied informally to anyone who rejected monasticism in favor of a vagabond or reclusive religious life. The terms *shami* and *hōshi* had similar implications, as did *shōnin,* the first character of which was sometimes the character for hijiri. The word *hijiri* also denotes special qualities of saintliness that regular monks did not necessarily possess. These qualities were incorporated in the concept of muen, as if the very involvement in structure obstructed one's pursuit of the Buddhist path.

Hijiri might include ordained monks retired or in retreat from regular clerical duties, hermits who had never troubled with ordination, or householders who periodically abandoned their fields and their families to embark on ascetic mountain pilgrimages. Though hijiri did live at temples, this was generally not a permanent arrangement; and most of the temples in question were isolated in the mountains and known for their encouragement of ascetic practice rather than for scholarship or rituals on behalf of the state.

Hijiri, like most nonelites, receive little attention in standard documentary sources, but setsuwa collections contain many striking portraits of them. One eleventh-century example is the setsuwa collection *Hokke genki*'s biography of Ninkyō, who studied at Tōdaiji and devoted himself to the Lotus sūtra (Inoue and Ōsone 1974:73–74; Dykstra 1983:45–46 [book 1, no. 16]). He began his ascetic life in summer retreats in the mountains and eventually developed supernatural powers enabling him to do such things as fill his water jar by telekinesis. At age eighty he retired permanently to Mt. Atago, west of Kyōto. Dressed in rags or deerskin and consuming only occasional bowls of gruel or cups of tea, he recited the sūtra constantly and lived to the age of 127. On his death he appeared in an old man's dreams, holding a copy of the sūtra and declaring that he was about to be reborn in Miroku's Tosotsu heaven.

Another example appears in both *Hokke genki* and the twelfth-century setsuwa collection *Konjaku monogatarishū*, although in this case the term *hōshi* is used instead of *hijiri* (Inoue and Ōsone 1974:142–144; Dykstra 1983:94–95 [book 2, no. 73]; Nagazumi and Ikegami 1966–1968, 2:161–164; translations from Ury 1979: 99–101 [book 15, no. 28]). In this tale a pilgrim-monk—a type of hijiri himself, though again the term is not used—lost his way in the mountains of Kyūshū but fortunately came upon a small hut. The woman who lived there reluctantly allowed him to stay the night. After dinner, a man appeared, carrying something: "The traveler saw that he was a priest (hōshi)—but with hair three or four inches long, dressed in rags. His appearance was horrifying: he was too filthy to come near." Not only that: when he sat down to eat what he had brought, the pilgrim discovered that it was the carrion of oxen and horses.

Later that evening the pilgrim heard his host get out of bed and leave the hut. Curious, the pilgrim followed, to discover a small chapel where his host performed the nenbutsu and Lotus sūtra readings. The next morning the host told his story to the visitor: "'Even though I was born in a human body and have become a priest, I shamelessly break the commandments, and when I die I shall fall into an evil path. . . . I inevitably sin in everything. For this reason, I seek out food that ordinary people won't even look at and prolong my existence while I long for the Buddha path.'" He finished the conversation by predicting the date of his death and (somewhat inconsistently) his rebirth in paradise.

On the appointed day the pilgrim-monk returned to seek out this unusual man, who indeed was on the brink of death. He and his female companion retired to the chapel and spent the night chanting the nenbutsu (praise to the Buddha's name). In the morning the hut was filled with radiant light and an "indescribable fragrance," clear indications that the couple had been welcomed into Amida's paradise.

Although the term *hijiri* is not used in this instance, the story clearly portrays aspects of the hijiri ideal. The two central characters both follow the hijiri path in their own ways. The traveler through whose eyes the episode is seen is no doubt an ordained monk who has abandoned the settled monastic life at least temporarily; his host probably never took Buddhist orders at all. A more fundamental point is the episode's definition of religious sincerity. Although the hōshi violated Buddhist prohibitions against eating meat and (apparently) having sexual relations (not to mention the societal taboo against eating carrion!), he turns out to be a genuinely sincere religious man. His consumption of carrion can even be interpreted as a virtuous act, since he is leaving better food for others. The story not only suggests the Buddhist concept that appearances are illusory, as Marian Ury points out (1979:12), but sets the relative values of following monastic and social regulations, on the one hand, and of pursuing sincere religious devotions, on the other.

The two setsuwa episodes cited here suggest that the hijiri ideal embraced seeming polar opposites. On the one hand, the hijiri was the perfect ascetic; on the other hand, he was the sincere religious practitioner who broke the rules. By this time it should be clear that it is much harder to explain what the hijiri were than what they were not. They were not regular monks in permanent residence at a temple, devoting their time to scholarship and temple ceremonies and their ambition to rising through the monastic hierarchy. Other than that it is difficult to define them, since their relationship with society at large was no more uniform than was their emphasis on ascetic discipline.

The term *hijiri* embraces two seemingly disparate modes of religious action: reclusion and evangelism. A hijiri might combine the lives of hermit and preacher, secluding himself in a mountain cave to fast and to meditate on a crude image he had carved himself, then emerging to exhort villagers to follow the Buddhist path. For example, the hijiri Genjō is portrayed in the *Hokke genki* as a hermit who retired to the mountains, on one occasion lived for a hundred days on a grain of millet per day, and consorted with boar, deer, bears, and wolves; however, he also actively preached among the people (Inoue and Ōsone 1974:144–145; Dykstra 1983:95–96 [book 2, no. 74]).

As hermit-ascetics, most hijiri followed the esoteric tradition that dominated both Shingon and Tendai: the attempt to reach buddhahood in one's present life through meditation, ritual, and magicoreligious formulae transmitted secretly from master to qualified disciple. As preachers, hijiri promoted simple practices that anyone could perform and goals that anyone could comprehend (see Inoue 1956:217–226). People learned to recite the nenbutsu, to cherish the Lotus sūtra not only as a sacred text but as a talisman with both magical and salvific powers, and to devote themselves to particular buddhas and bodhisattvas such as Jizō, who had promised to rescue sinners from hell. The spiritual goal advanced by hijiri was not described as nirvana, a state that must have seemed uncomfortably like extinction, but as rebirth in a paradise painted in concrete, physical terms.

Hijiri, moreover, promoted a type of Buddhism that answered the mundane needs of ordinary people as well as their spiritual aims. The religious practices that hijiri taught the common folk were laced with magic and ritual designed to make crops and people prosper. Moreover, though often lowborn and illiterate—in contrast to scholarly regular monks—hijiri were skilled in such tasks as building bridges and digging wells. Thus they were often of practical use to their followers. For reasons such as these, it was largely through the efforts of hijiri that Buddhism entered the popular consciousness and wove itself into pre-Buddhist beliefs.

Hijiri were the heirs of such shami as Shingyō and Hōkyō, portrayed in the *Nihon ryōiki,* but especially of Gyōki, who had become a folk hero known for his compassion, his wisdom, and his working of miracles. His activities as a founder of temples—he is credited with forty-nine—and his skill as a builder of bridges, roads, and irrigation canals also captured the popular imagination. In this guise Gyōki appears in almost all important setsuwa collections. According to the *Hokke genki,* Gyōki was skilled in construction work that benefited the populace: "After studying how paddy fields should be farmed and irrigated, he dug ponds for reservoirs and built irrigation dikes. Hearing of this, the people came to help him, and the jobs were finished in no time at all. Even now, farmers reap the benefits of his projects" (Inoue and Ōsone 1974:51–52 [book 1, no. 2]; see also the translation in Dykstra 1983:27–29).

Curiously, it was not until the Kamakura period that Gyōki emerged in the common view as the Tōdaiji kanjin hijiri, though a popular but apocryphal tale in the tenth-century *Sanbōekotoba* links him with the temple's dedication in 752, some three years after his actual death. The tale reports that Shōmu asked him to lecture at the Tōdaiji dedication. He modestly declined the invitation but served as head of the welcoming committee for the Indian monk Bodhisena, who was given the honor instead (Minamoto 1982, 1:180–181; Kamens 1988:198–199 [book 2, no. 3]).

Few Heian period hijiri rose to attract the imperial attention that Gyōki did, however. Most simply inhabited the fringes of the monastic world, lodging in small temples in commoner neighborhoods or in the mountains, or simply wandering from place to place (Nakanodō 1970:417–418). Sometimes hijiri built temples themselves with popular support. The tenth-century hijiri Kūya, for example, established Rokuharamitsuji in Kyōto. Others sought donations for large monasteries in return for room and board at one of their branch temples. Hijiri often referred to themselves as muen, a term that described their vagabond status and their lack of permanent connections to any single institution.

The twelfth-century tale collection *Shūi ōjōden* describes one such hijiri, a man named Zenpō: "He wandered through the provinces and villages without a fixed abode, always dressed in shabby, soiled clothing. He collected alms from monks and lay believers and lectured on the sūtras" (Inoue and Ōsone 1974:385 [book 3, no. 27])." Another example appears in the tale collection *Honchō shinshū ōjōden* (Inoue and Ōsone 1974:691 [no. 34]). This story tells of Dōjaku (d. 1147), called the Iga hijiri because he was from Iga province. Dōjaku retired from his life as a layman and began a lengthy pilgrimage to holy mountains and famous temples in neighboring Yamato. Eventually he arrived at Gangōji, where he sat in meditation and practiced the nenbutsu. Subsequently he moved to another temple, where he solicited donations for one thousand images of Kannon—probably small wooden figures or woodblock prints. Later on, "mustering all his ability and never ceasing his efforts, even for a day," he collected donations to have three giant bells cast, giving one to Tōdaiji, one to Hasedera, and one to the temple at the holy mountain of Kinpusen.

Like Zenpō, kanjin hijiri were mostly of low status: unordained, unattached, and unschooled. They were temporarily employed by temples for kanjin activities, perhaps moving as a group from temple to temple. Their presence was not always welcomed by the regular monks. A document dated 1075, issued by the Tōji branch temple Chinkōji in Kyōto, complains of a group of hijiri hired by the temple's *bettō* (administrator). Attempting to collect donations for the repair of a pagoda—possibly at Tōji rather than at Chinkōji itself—the hijiri pestered even the Chinkōji monks: "In the past three years they have paced back and forth on the road in front [of the temple], practicing ascetic rituals and pressing the monks to give them donations, saying, "If you'll only add a speck of dust—!" (Takeuchi 1963–1976, 3:1122–1125 [doc. 1110]).

Although the complaint clearly had political motivations— the bettō was an outsider appointed to the post against the wishes of the local monks themselves—the description of the hijiri and their kanjin activities hints that they were an extortionate lot, beyond the pale of monkish respectability. This description may be a reflection of educated monks' prejudice against those of modest social origins: even though they freed regular monks from the demeaning but necessary work of begging for contributions, hijiri were probably despised by their monastic "betters."

Heian period kanjin hijiri collected donations for a variety of projects, such as repairing temple buildings, making images, or copying sūtras. According to the tenth-century literary anthology *Honchō monzui,* the Amidist hijiri Kūya, to fulfill his vow to have the Dai Hannya sūtra copied, asked people for tiny contributions —"half a penny or a speck of dust" (Kakimura 1968, 2:891; Horiike 1976:6). Secular public works projects were also supported by kanjin donations: an episode in *Konjaku monogatarishū* tells of a hijiri—modeled, perhaps, on Gyōki—who canvassed villagers to rebuild a dilapidated bridge (Nagazumi and Ikegami 1966–1968, 6:188 [book 31, no. 2]).

Contemporary sources suggest some ways in which the hijiri worked. The band at Chinkōji paced back and forth in front of the temple, no doubt entreating passersby as well as the monks themselves. Representatives of Mandaraji in Sanuki province traveled from village to village, collecting individual donations and recording the names of givers in a rollbook (Takeuchi 1963–1976, 3:1089, 1109 [docs. 1077, 1088]). Most Heian kanjin efforts were small-scale and local, however (Kawakatsu 1971:58), and the Mandaraji project, which ranged over several provinces, seems to have been atypical for the age. Far more common were cases in which hijiri collected a few donations for a limited project.

The Copying and Burial of Sūtras

Kanjin hijiri were particularly active in securing donations for the copying of sūtras. Compared to some of the other projects funded by kanjin campaigns, sūtra copying was probably inexpensive; thus it could be accomplished by securing donations from a relatively small number of people. Donors included ordinary villagers as well as aristocrats, and provincials as well as residents of the capital. For example, in 1115 and 1116, the kanjin monk (sō) Shōken sought donations to support the copying of sūtras for the collection at Hōryūji (Takeuchi 1963–1976, 13:169–171 [docs. 943, 948, 955]). Shōken's name appears as kanjin sō on three sūtras, one donated by a rural notable, one by an official of the Imperial Storehouse Bureau, and one by a village *kechienshu* (donors' group).

Copying sūtras was thought to be a particularly efficacious way to secure salvation for oneself, or for others through the transfer of merit. Dedications of the Hōryūji sūtras indicate that the act of copying would benefit not only the donors and their families, but everyone else as well: "This has been done to secure rebirth in the Gokuraku paradise for our ancestors and benefactors, to fulfill their prayers in this world and the next, and to bring spiritual benefits equally to all creatures" (Takeuchi 1963–1976, 13:170 [doc. 948]).

Sometimes people preserved sūtras for the future by burying them in the ground, an activity that was often funded by kanjin efforts. The first known sūtra burial was sponsored in 1007 by the illustrious Fujiwara Michinaga, the power behind the throne, whose inscription expressed the hope that upon the advent of Miroku the future Buddha, the sūtras would emerge from the earth and help to convert the congregation present (Nara Kokuritsu Hakubutsukan 1973: no. 1). During the next two centuries, many sūtras were either inserted in copper tubes for burial or inscribed on tile or stone. The effort to preserve them was often linked directly to Miroku's advent and the hope for the future that it promised; even when this purpose was not explicitly stated, it seems likely that it was kept in mind by donors and kanjin hijiri.

Though some sūtra burials were sponsored by the most powerful among the nobility, others were the work of provincials of much lower rank. For example, in 1083 a donors' group from provincial notable families named Kiyohara, Usa, and Fujiwara had a copy of the Lotus sūtra buried at Rokugosan Suigetsuji in Bungo province (Takeuchi 1963–1976, 12:133–134 [doc. 132]). In 1103 a layman from Yamashiro province assumed the guise of a monk and wandered among the people, collecting from "some ten thousands" in order to copy the Lotus sūtra, which was then buried at a Kai province site (Sasaki 1987:16–17). Such examples suggest that kanjin hijiri rapidly spread the practice of sūtra burial throughout the populace, who responded with donations according to their means. It also seems that hijiri worked closely with metal casters who made the copper casings in which the sūtras were placed (Nakanodō 1970:418). This close association between kanjin hijiri and artisans continued throughout the Kamakura period.

Kanjin and Temple Building

The practice of kanjin accommodated both temples and muen hijiri: temples received income without expending the efforts of their regular monks, and hijiri found a means of support that they could combine with solitary meditation and asceticism. Yet there must have been disadvantages in a system that permitted so much independence for the hijiri. Receipts must have been hard to predict or control, and temples could never be sure that the hijiri were keeping only the agreed-upon percentage. If major projects were to be funded through kanjin campaigns, temples had to manage these campaigns more firmly.

Temples regularized the kanjin process in several ways in the late Heian and Kamakura periods. Some relied on their own monks to supervise the campaigns and sometimes even to do the legwork themselves. Written requests were issued, stating the projects for which donations were intended, and were presumably circulated to potential givers. Temple offices, in some cases permanent ones, were established to oversee kanjin efforts, and the cooperation of court, shogunate, provincial officials, and shōen proprietors was actively sought. Using these methods, temples were able to finance even costly construction projects in part through kanjin campaigns.

A major campaign of the Heian period was conducted in the late eleventh century by Mandaraji in Sanuki province, a branch temple of the great Kyōto monastery Tōji (Takeuchi 1963–1976, 3:1089, 1109 [docs. 1077, 1088]; *Kagawa ken no chimei* 1989:374–375). The project began in 1058 when a monk named Zenban (or Zenbō)—perhaps a muen hijiri—visited the temple, said to have been founded by the Shingon patriarch Kūkai, and lamented its dilapidated state. Zenban settled at Mandaraji, vowing to rebuild it, and by 1072 had collected some donations and entered contributors' names in a rollbook. Mandaraji's overall financial condition, however, was extremely unstable. Even though the temple had been granted tax exemptions, these privileges were frequently ignored by local authorities, and others encroached on some of the temple's fields. Moreover, Mandaraji shared a bettō with its neighbor Zentsūji, also a Tōji branch. Zenban complained to the main temple that the bettō had seized Mandaraji materials and diverted them to Zentsūji, making it impossible to complete the construction project.

Later in 1072, Zenban sent another petition to Tōji, declaring that, although he had solicited donations in various provinces, he had not received enough to meet his needs. With the help of the provincial governor's office, the main temple scrambled to make up the shortfall, and Mandaraji was given firmer control over its lands and laborers. Thus, the lecture hall, the main hall, an auxiliary chapel, the monks' residence, and the graveyard chapel were all rebuilt. Zenban himself administered the project, supervising the transport of logs and the hiring of artisans.

The story of Mandaraji's reconstruction suggests the increasing importance kanjin campaigns were assuming in temples' financial lives as well as the degree to which temples competed for scarce resources. Such competition plagued other temples as well: Tōji itself was the defendant in a suit filed by monks of Mt. Kōya, who accused the head temple of the Shingon school of diverting materials collected in an 1174 campaign for services of its own (Takeuchi 1963–1976, 7:2842–2843 [doc. 3668]).

However, Mandaraji's plight outlined in Zenban's second petition illustrates that kanjin methods were inadequate to meet all the expenses of a major project. Other temples that collected donations through kanjin means, moreover, repeatedly complained of shortfalls, yet continued to venture campaigns. This raises the question of motivation: if kanjin campaigns were only marginally productive, then why did temples conduct them at all? As I will argue in detail in the next chapter, the answer probably lies in the nature of kanjin campaigns as efforts to convert the populace. They could be justified by either economic or religious aims —which, in fact, were virtually impossible to separate, since a temple's financial health was critical for its religious mission.

Zenban himself is typical of kanjin hijiri in the late Heian and Kamakura periods. Whether he was originally a muen hijiri or just a monk from another temple, he was an outsider to begin with; the charismatic stranger who restores ruined temples is a standard figure in kanjin campaigns. Moreover, he supervised the entire construction project, much as Chōgen did at Tōdaiji some two centuries later; and, like Chōgen, he concerned himself with general temple finances as well as the construction project at hand. Such concentration of responsibility in the hands of the kanjin hijiri is generally considered characteristic of Kamakura kanjin efforts rather than of those of earlier periods (Nakanodō 1970: 407–409). Yet it should be recalled that in setsuwa episodes, Heian period hijiri built bridges and dug irrigation ditches as well as collecting donations for them. If these tales reflect reality, then the broad responsibilities of Chōgen and Zenban were based on earlier Heian precedents.

The Mandaraji evidence suggests that we do not have to wait until the Kamakura period for ambitious building projects funded at least in part by kanjin means. Another example is the project undertaken in 1137 by the small temple Komatsudera in Kawachi province to reconstruct buildings destroyed in a typhoon. The destruction of the temple is described by *Kawachi no kuni Komatsudera engi*:[2] "On the twelfth day of the ninth month of the fifth year of Daiji [1130], a typhoon blew down from the heavens. Provinces, villages, mountains, temples, chapels, and monks' lodgings could not escape destruction from the wind. At our temple, the Golden Hall, the pagoda, the belltower, the sūtra repository, and the main gate were all blown to pieces" (1927:305–307).The text continues on a more cheerful note, explaining that seven years later the monk Kan'en addressed the other temple monks, urging them to canvass the public for donations to repair the buildings and restore images and sūtras. A young woman of the Minamoto family, who lived in Eguchi village, pledged a substantial donation. Others gave as well, in response to Kan'en's appeal, which asked for "a small tool or a scrap of wood" for the project, and promised to pray for the donors' enlightenment in their subsequent lives. The *hōgachō* (donation rollbook) attached, dated 1139, lists seventy-seven gifts of cash, rice, and horses, as well as small gifts—too numerous to mention—of the "small tool or scrap of wood" variety. Donors are listed by name, village, office or social status, and gift. The majority of donors with identifiable residences lived in villages in the same region of Kawachi as the temple.

Evidence from the late Heian period suggests that not all kanjin campaigns were ad hoc efforts, but some were carefully planned and executed by solicitors of considerable sophistication. Zenban's ability to attract help from the provincial government indicates that he was a man of some status and influence. In another case, when the kanjin solicitor Sairen sought donations for the casting of a bath cauldron and a bell at Kōrōji in Iga province in 1140 (Takeuchi 1963–1976, 11:300–301 [supp. doc. 315]), he issued an appeal written in classical Chinese; while he may have been either a Kōrōji monk or a muen hijiri, he was clearly a highly educated man. The very existence of a document suggests a degree of formality, systemization, and orderly keeping of records. Another indication of regularity is the creation of temple offices, *daikanjinshiki*, which held responsibility for campaigns. The earliest example I have found so far is dated 1154, when the retired emperor Toba appointed a monk named Enshō to that post at Nenbutsu Sanmaiin at Shitennōji, a major temple in Izumi province (Takeuchi 1963–1976, 11:309, 337 [supp. docs. 328, 384]). It is not certain what the post entailed, but the term is a legal one, indicating in this case an office with certain rights and duties. Enshō was given jurisdiction over temple offices and the administrative affairs of temple shōen, suggesting that he had broad responsibilities for financial matters.

The increase in both the frequency and regularity of kanjin campaigns can be explained in part by economic developments in the Heian period, particularly its later years. These developments provided motivation and opportunity for kanjin campaigns not only by making them profitable, but by engendering a new way of thinking about the economy that permitted gifts to be used in pragmatic and productive ways.

Kanjin and the Late Heian Economy

By the late Heian period kanjin campaigns had become a regular function of temples and a standard method to supplement income from agricultural land. This phenomenon implies that substantial numbers of donors had surplus income to give to temples and that the late Heian economy was expanding rather than stagnant. Since this latter proposition flies in the face of much conventional wisdom about the period, it is worth examining in some detail. It will be helpful to draw comparisons with medieval Europe, where similar religious phenomena were associated with economic growth.

It is generally accepted that sometime between the late Heian and the late Kamakura periods, the Japanese economy changed in several fundamental ways (Koizumi 1975:127–131; Wakita 1975: 322–333). To begin with, productivity was increased by land reclamation, doublecropping, and the use of draft animals. This increase produced a surplus that promoted the growth of village commerce. Commerce encouraged the development of a standard medium of exchange, and by the thirteenth century cash—in use in Nara and early Heian times but largely out of circulation by the eleventh century—was employed to purchase land and pay taxes. Although the thirteenth-century economy was by no means completely monetized, even peasants in remote regions were becoming accustomed to cash. There is evidence of its use even in remote Mutsu province by 1240 (Mori 1973:28).

Though most scholars accept this general picture, there is considerable disagreement on timing. There are those, such as Nagahara Keiji, who argue that the development of markets and the use of money were Kamakura period phenomena, dependent on such circumstances as the bakufu's dispatch of jitō to supervise the shōen (especially after 1221, when the Jōkyū uprising necessitated firm bakufu controls over land), an increase in lawsuits over land rights, and the consequent growth of traffic and the exchange of goods (1970:79–80). Nagahara also maintains that, even in the twelfth and thirteenth centuries, agricultural production was unstable, and fields were often allowed to go out of cultivation (1968:160). In other words, he depicts the economy of the late Heian and early Kamakura periods as stagnant and locally self-sufficient.

Other scholars suggest a more dynamic picture for the earlier period. For example, Inagaki Yasuhiko argues that the productivity of existing fields was improved substantially in the late Heian period, especially in the Kinai (1975:168–182). According to Inagaki, the increase was due to small-scale land reclamation projects, efforts to keep arable land from going out of cultivation in time of drought or other disaster, and land management methods that encouraged the cultivation of even marginal fields. Most viable projects were modest ones that could be managed by local magnates and thus enhance their wealth and power. Methods of tax farming—which put control of land and labor into local hands —were also employed on both shōen and public lands. In addition, projects were sometimes carried out by peasant cooperative groups: for example, in the Kanji era (1087–1094) in Iga province, peasants from the Tōdaiji shōen Kuroda moved onto land originally reclaimed by a Gangōji monk. There they built irrigation ponds to divert river water, replacing an irrigation system that had used natural spring and mountain water. By the end of the twelfth century, a cultivated area of seventeen *chō* (roughly fifty acres) had grown to sixty chō. Inagaki argues that the project must have required official assistance but was managed by local residents. Projects such as these probably supported an expanding population even before the Kamakura period changes that Nagahara credits with economic growth.

If Inagaki's arguments are valid, some of the fruits of these projects remained in local hands; otherwise there would have been little motivation for people to engage in such expensive undertakings. This surplus, moreover, must have facilitated the growth of local markets and stimulated the development of an appropriate medium of exchange.

Coins actually had been minted in Japan in the Nara and early Heian periods, but the use of money could not have penetrated very deeply into society. Local economies were largely self-sufficient, and the court could simply demand that provincial subordinates send them special products—textiles, for example, or dried fish. As the shōen system developed, however, it seems that proprietors often received more goods than their households could use; thus these goods were sold for a profit at Kyōto markets (Mori 1973:18–22). Evidence from *Konjaku monogatarishū* indicates a lively commercial exchange between Kyōto and the provinces

(Mori 1973:23; Nagazumi and Ikegami 1966–1968, 6:109–112 [book 29, no. 36]). This exchange seems to have taken place around the same time, the late eleventh century, that (in Inagaki's view) local agricultural productivity was rising. Ironically, it was just about that time that coins minted in Japan had largely gone out of circulation for a variety of reasons, including a shortage of copper and the problem of counterfeiting (Takizawa 1970:3–7). Since the end of the tenth century, however, coins from Sung dynasty China had been available to the Japanese. There is almost no documentary evidence of cash transactions from the end of the eleventh century until the mid-twelfth, although Takizawa Takeo argues that the private use of currency probably continued even during this period (1970:12). In the mid-twelfth century, however, cash transactions reappear in the documents: land was sold for cash in 1150 in Yamato province, in 1162 at an unnamed place (but probably Yamashiro), and in 1176 in Kyōto (Mori 1973:27). It seems likely that Sung coins were used in these transactions.

Evidence from kanjin campaigns, though very scanty, also points to the use of cash in the mid-twelfth century. In 1151 thirty-three donors contributed amounts ranging from thirty to fifty units of cash (the denomination is not specified) for the carving of an image of Shakyamuni at Hōrakuji in Tosa province (Takeuchi 1963–1976, 6:2283 [doc. 2736]). The list was placed inside the statue, a common storage place for documents of this type. Donors included laymen, lay women, and monks; several surnames are listed, but about half are of the Saeki family, an old court family that had taken root in Shikoku by the end of the eighth century. The rollbook recording donations to Komatsudera lists fifty-eight cash gifts, some of them quite substantial (*Kawachi no kuni Komatsudera engi* 1927:305–307). Although it has been suggested that the Komatsudera records are not completely authentic, the very simplicity of the Hōrakuji document implies *its* veracity. A listing of names and donations, it appears to be a hastily scribbled note, perhaps by the kanjin monk himself.

In summary, scattered pieces of evidence indicate that by the middle of the twelfth century an economic revolution—involving increases in agricultural productivity and the use of money—was already well under way. It also appears that religious institutions, always sensitive to their own financial situation, took steps to exploit this revolution. Those institutions important enough to be shōen proprietors could profit from an increase in yields and a chance to market their own surplus proceeds. These and other institutions—provincial temples or lesser temples in Nara or Kyōto—also may have found it beneficial to tap a new source of support: the rural middle class of managers and prosperous cultivators. The new economic situation may help to explain the decisions of temples to conduct kanjin campaigns for major projects in the late eleventh and twelfth centuries. That kanjin campaigns were conducted in provincial locations such as Sanuki, Kawachi, Iga, and Tosa suggests that, as productivity increased, some provincial residents accrued a surplus that they could donate to temples.

Marc Bloch argues that in Europe in the mid-eleventh century there occurred an economic revolution marked by population growth, the development of a commercial economy, the appearance of cities and an urban middle class, and the transformation of forest and wasteland into cultivated land (1961:69–70). This revolution in some ways resembles that in late Heian Japan. Europe of the eleventh and twelfth centuries also witnessed religious phenomena similar to those in Japan of the same period: hermits who were also evangelists, a rash of church construction, and public campaigns for donations to support that construction.

In contrast to the completely reclusive desert fathers of early Christianity, medieval European hermits worked among the people. It is thus difficult to define them as hermits, although that is the term in common use for them. According to Henrietta Leyser: "[Hermits] are not expected to try to reform the world, to become wandering preachers, to take upon themselves the care of lepers, prostitutes, the sick and the poor, to proclaim by word and deed that most existing ecclesiastical institutions were at worst rotten, at best inadequate. But this is what the new hermits of the eleventh and twelfth centuries did" (1984:1–2).

Medieval European equivalents of the hijiri included Bernard of Tiron (ca. 1046–1117), who wandered through France preaching in villages and cities and at castles, and Robert of Arbrissel (ca. 1055–1117), who preached among the poor, especially prostitutes, and established leper colonies. Regular monks objected to the hermits, complaining that they were unkempt and unrespectable, that they unjustly criticized both monks and the secular clergy, and that they wandered about "trying to attract attention and donations" (Little 1978:76–83). No doubt these monks would have sympathized with the regular clergy at Chinkōji. Hermits' active involvement in charity and preaching, and their willingness to perform manual labor, however, brought them close to the people and won them lay patrons (Leyser 1984: 59–81).

The eleventh and twelfth centuries were also a period of rapid church construction. Part of the reason may be that labor and materials were readily available: as Christopher Brooke points out, construction in Europe initially made use of the chronically underemployed labor that characterized subsistence agricultural society (1987:73–74). The search for means to pay for the projects resulted in economic growth. This process probably occurred in Japan as well, and the late-Heian development of village commerce and small-scale land reclamation that promoted temple building was no doubt further stimulated by demands for materials and labor for these construction projects.

Church construction in medieval Europe was supported at times by public subscription campaigns. One campaign occurred in England in the late twelfth century, when donations were sought to rebuild St. Paul's cathedral in London (Graham 1945– 1947:73–76). Those who subscribed to the fund or remembered it in their wills were rewarded with masses sung on their behalf by the priests of the diocese. Even if a donor died in mortal sin, he or she was promised burial in consecrated ground. Like the donors to the Komatsudera reconstruction in twelfth-century Japan, those who supported St. Paul's were offered rewards in their next life in return for their gifts. Lester Little sees such phenomena as indications of the development of a profit economy (1978:29–32).

Little contrasts the profit economy in medieval Europe with the gift economy that preceded it (1978:3–6). In the sixth century a Burgundian king found a cache of gold, which he "fashioned into an altar canopy of wondrous size and great weight"; thwarted in his plan to send the canopy to the holy sepulchre in Jerusalem, the king gave it to a nearby church. In contrast, when tenth-century workmen unearthed a large store of gold while preparing to build a cathedral, the bishop at the head of the construction effort "rendered thanks to God, and then had [the gold] all assigned to the construction project." "In the first instance," Little explains, "the reconversion of treasure into yet another form of treasure is typical of the gift economy that flourished in the centuries following the Germanic migrations. The exchange of treasure for building materials and labour in the second instance, however, signals new modes of thought and behaviour . . ." In a gift economy, goods and services are not assigned specific value, and the act of exchange is more important than the items exchanged. Coins, if they exist, are used as treasure—hoarded, displayed, or buried. In a profit economy, coins are used as money—as a tool to pay for goods and services that have set values. There is no hard line, of course, between the two types of economy: values can fluctuate in a profit economy, for example, in the practice of bargaining, and a gift requires one in return, usually of equal or greater value. This requirement holds even when the recipients are deities or the dead, to whom gifts are offered in anticipation "of a very real, indeed essential, return" (Little 1978:4).

The increasing frequency of kanjin campaigns in late Heian Japan suggests that there, too, a profit economy was beginning to take hold. The use of money may, in fact, have been encouraged by kanjin hijiri; if not, the flexibility and convenience of money would certainly have made it welcome.

Yet there was an ambivalent attitude toward the use of money that underscores the transitional nature of late Heian kanjin campaigns. Coins that fell into the possession of temples were not necessarily meant to be used as cash. The earliest Sung coins imported into Japan often found their way to temples, but they were probably meant to be kept as treasure, not spent to meet expenses. Archaeologists have found coins in small numbers at late Heian ritual sites: temples and shrines, graves, and mounds where sūtras were buried (Yashima 1959:167–168). Devout Chinese Buddhists placed coins inside an image of Shakyamuni sent to Japan in 983 and later enshrined at Saga Seiryōji in Kyōto (Mori 1973:25). It appears that such coins had ritual rather than monetary value; thus their function was similar to that of the weapons and pottery found in prehistoric graves. Coins given to a temple in response to a kanjin campaign, however, were probably intended to serve as money, since kanjin requests usually asked for donations to finance particular projects. The difference between the coins in the Seiryōji image and those donated to kanjin efforts heralds an important change not only in the economy of late

Heian Japan but also in the way in which people conceived of that economy. Donations to temples, in fact, link the two modes of thinking about exchange that Little has described for medieval Europe. In late Heian Japan, kanjin campaigns partook of both the gift and the profit economies. People offered temples cash donations—just as they had offered rice or other goods—in return for promises of salvation (the "essential return" that Little argues was expected for offerings to deities). Kanjin hijiri, in fact, committed the buddhas in advance to repay donors with rebirth in paradise or other spiritual benefits, no matter how small the gift. The promise of uniform benefit in itself suggests that it was the thought, not the amount, that mattered, an essential ingredient of gift economy thinking. At the same time, both hijiri and donors were aware that gifts would be pooled and spent to finance specific projects; these projects were generally announced in the kanjin appeal. To be successful, kanjin campaigns had to be motivated by profit economy thinking, which saw money primarily as a tool to meet the expenses of timber, tile, and labor, while the promise of salvation remained without a set value, lest giving be discouraged and the essential religious purpose of kanjin campaigns be destroyed. The skill of kanjin hijiri in negotiating this narrow transitional path permitted their temples to find support outside the shōen system and offered the promise of Buddhist salvation to far greater numbers of people than had ever hoped for it before.

By the end of the Heian period, both temples and state authorities had discovered that kanjin could be a useful tool for extending their power and influence. The characteristic of kanjin campaigns that made them so useful was that donations were perceived to be voluntary. They may not always have been so, especially when political authorities added their imprimatur to a campaign. Yet the perception that people donated willingly to kanjin campaigns implied that they also willingly accepted the authority of the temples that conducted them and the lay powers that supported them, a valuable tool for both temples and political leaders. Put in somewhat different terms, religious and lay authorities tried to persuade people that they were bound not by hierarchy and compulsion, but by the ties of communitas.

It would not be accurate, however, to look at kanjin as a cynical effort to keep people under control. A close examination indicates that the monks and hijiri who conceived, planned, and executed kanjin campaigns did so with the spiritual welfare of donors in mind as well as the welfare of the temple. These benefits could be equated in the view of the monks involved in the revival of Nara Buddhism in the twelfth and thirteenth centuries; the link between the two was the temple's need for the wherewithal to carry out its religious mission. Thus Nara monks had strong religious motivations to seek donations from the public. In the next chapter, I will examine these motivations, along with the aims, appeals, and methods of a typical kanjin campaign that spanned the transition from the Heian to the Kamakura age.

Three

ALMS FOR KASAGI TEMPLE

The dedication of a small offering shall without fail enable you to see the Buddha, hear his teachings, aim at enlightenment, and fulfill that aim. —Sōshō 1960:238.

Thus in 1196 the distinguished Nara monk Jōkei sought donations for rites to dedicate relics of the Buddha at Kasagidera, the small mountain temple to which he had retreated several years before. The 1196 request was part of a kanjin campaign conducted by the temple between 1182 and 1203. The campaign was intended to revitalize the temple, and donations were earmarked for religious services, new images, building repair and construction, and the support of monks' daily lives.

In exploring the Kasagidera effort, I have two purposes: first, to examine the aims, methods, solicitors, and donors of a representative campaign that spanned the end of the Heian and the beginning of the Kamakura period and, second, to assess the role of kanjin campaigns in the revival of Nara Buddhism. I chose the Kasagidera campaign for several reasons. While both large and small temples conducted kanjin campaigns, it was the small, financially insecure ones such as Kasagidera that did so the most frequently. The campaign, furthermore, is comparatively well documented for one of its type. Eight written requests for donations have been preserved in *Miroku nyorai kannōshō,* compiled by the thirteenth-century Tōdaiji monk Sōshō (1960:234–243). Although it is not difficult to find information on the kanjin efforts of large, powerful temples, most small temples' campaigns are documented by one written request at best. More often, we learn of their kanjin efforts through laconic inscriptions on images or references in documents that pertain to other matters. The Kasagidera requests, explicit on the goals, methods, and religious motivations of the campaign, can help us to assess similar factors in other kanjin efforts. In addition, Kasagidera's campaign occurred at an important transitional time in Japanese history. The years between 1182 and 1203 embraced the Genpei war, in which warriors led by Minamoto Yoritomo defeated their rivals to become the paramount military clan in Japan, and Yoritomo's establishment of a warrior government, the Kamakura bakufu, as a parallel structure to the civilian government of the emperor and his court. Once the bakufu became a decisive force in land tenure decisions, temples had new patrons to solicit (and to please) as well as a more complex situation on the shōen that necessitated the search for these patrons. Kasagidera's campaign in this transitional time was itself transitional in nature: sharing elements of both small-scale efforts and large, organized, publicly recognized campaigns conducted by major temples, it can help to shed light on both.

Finally, Kasagidera was one of many small temples that maintained close ties with the great Buddhist institutions of Nara and their monks, including activists in the Nara revival movement. The temple's *honzon* (main image) was of Miroku, one focus of the revival. Nara monks retreated to Kasagi for meditation and ascetic practice, and Jōkei, a leader of the revival, secluded himself there for fifteen years, taking charge of the kanjin campaign. Examining the kanjin campaign in which Jōkei played so large a part can help to explain both the thinking of this seminal figure in the Nara revival and the ideology of the revival movement.

The appropriation of kanjin means by leaders of the Nara revival adds significance to the kanjin campaign as a method of transmitting Buddhist teachings. The connection between alms collection and the revival movement rests on three interconnected elements in medieval Japanese Buddhist doctrine and practice: the concepts of *hōben* and restoration, and the emphasis on community among monks and lay believers.

Hōben, or expedient means, according to the Lotus sūtra and other texts, was the principle that stipulated different religious practices for those at different stages of spiritual development. Any practice that guided a person along the path to Buddhist enlightenment was justified as hōben, no matter how indulgent or even bizarre it might seem to most observers. Hōben legitimized religious eclecticism, permitting revivalist leaders both to demand of themselves strict adherence to the precepts that bound the clergy and to reach out to lay believers by advocating simple means of obtaining salvation.

The concept of restoration is also crucial to understanding the way that Nara revival monks employed the kanjin campaign. The monks were attempting, first of all, to restore the purity and the power of Buddhism that they believed had existed in Shakyamuni's day. This task involved the restoration of monastic virtue (the precepts), the construction and reconstruction of Buddhism's physical edifice (temples), and the creation of a community that included the simplest lay believer as well as the most sophisticated and virtuous monk. The need for restoration must have seemed acute in the late twelfth century, when political and economic changes created both challenge and opportunity for the Nara monasteries, heretofore able to rely on their old aristocratic connections.

Victor Turner has correlated societal crisis, the genesis of religions, and communitas (1974:250–251). He points out that "under favorable circumstances some structural form, generated long ago from a moment of communitas, may be almost miraculously liquefied into a living form of communitas again. This is what revitalistic or revivalistic religious movements . . . aim to do —to restore the social bond of their communicants to the pristine vigor of that religion in its days of generative crisis and ecstasy."

In attempting to restore the Buddhism of Shakyamuni's day, the Nara monks were aiming at the regeneration of communitas within the "structural form" of organized religion. This aim is evidenced by the stress on community within the monastic organization—the deepest meaning, perhaps, of the emphasis on the precepts that bound monk to monk. It can also be seen in the attempt to broaden that community to include all humankind, the ultimate aim of kanjin campaigns.

The Temple in History and Legend

Kasagidera is located about twelve miles northeast of Nara in southern Yamashiro province. Atop Kasagi mountain, which overlooks the Kizu river that flows to Nara, the temple was isolated from the great urban monasteries but accessible to their monks. Kasagidera was founded, according to legend, when heavenly beings engraved an image of Miroku on a cliff at the mountain. According to the version of this tale that appears in the twelfth-century collection *Konjaku monogatarishū,* Prince Ōtomo (648–672), hunting on horseback in the mountains, suddenly found himself trapped on a ledge so narrow that he could neither dismount nor turn his horse around. Expecting to die, the prince was seized with fear:

Lamenting, he said, "If you are here, kami of the mountain, please save my life. If you do I will carve an image of Miroku on the face of this cliff." Then, in response to his prayer, the kami enabled the horse to back out of the narrow place to a wider spot. The prince dismounted and tearfully fell on his knees to pray. So that he could find the place later, he took off the hemp hat that he had been wearing and put it down, and then he returned home. One or two days later, he went back to find his hat. Descending from the mountaintop, he skirted the cliff and arrived at its foot. He looked upward, but his view could not reach the top of the cliff, which seemed to be lost in the clouds. With anguish in his heart, the prince gazed at the cliff, realizing that he could not carve an image of Miroku on its face. Then heavenly beings took pity on him and helped him. While a black cloud obscured everything and made it dark as night, they carved the Buddha in an instant. In the darkness the prince could hear the spatter of many small stones. Presently the cloud lifted, the mist cleared, and the sky brightened. When the prince gazed up at the cliff, he saw a splendid image of Miroku engraved there. (Nagazumi and Ikegami 1966–1968:88–90 [book 11, no. 30])

The legend explains both the name of the mountain and its temple ("hemp hat" [*kasa*] plus "to put" [*oki*] becomes Kasagi) and the engraving of the image, exalting temple and image through connections to the imperial family and to supernatural beings. The image was destroyed when battle fires scorched the cliff in the fourteenth century, but its alcove remains, attesting to its size (fifteen meters in height). Kamakura period copies in painting and sculpture indicate that the figure stood on a lotus-petal platform, its hands making signs *(mudrā)* of comfort and reassurance. The image, which apparently portrayed Miroku as a buddha rather than as a bodhisattva, signified Miroku's future mission of salvation. Art historians (e.g., Shimizu 1973:97) have determined that the image actually dates from the eighth century, and it seems likely that the temple was founded at the same time.

Kasagidera's mountain location made it an important center of Shugendō (mountain ascetic practice). Generally speaking, mountains were regarded as sacred in the pre-Buddhist Japanese tradition—perhaps for their grandeur, perhaps because they were the source of streams that fed the rice fields, perhaps because they were mysterious and dangerous, and thus thought to be the homes of numina called kami. When temples were built in the mountains, they borrowed this sanctity and added it to their own as Buddhist holy places. This process may be one meaning represented by Kasagidera's founding legend, in which the kami's compassionate deed compels an act of Buddhist faith in response.

The sanctity of physical locations was often enhanced by a process of identification, in which the kami of a place was said to be a particular buddha or bodhisattva or the place itself was said to be a mandala or a Buddhist heaven.[1] Hijiri were drawn to Kasagi mountain because it was in itself regarded as sacred space, just as were other nearby mountains such as Kinpu, Kumano, and Ōmine. By the early Kamakura period, in fact, Kasagi and Kinpu were identified in at least one Shugendō source with the outer and inner realms of Miroku's Tosotsu heaven as well as with the *taizō-kai* (womb-store world) and the *kongōkai* (diamond world), the two halves of the universe as depicted in the mandala of esoteric Buddhism (Sakurai, Hagiwara, and Miyata 1975:136–139).[2] According to the source in question, a collection of lore and traditions called *Shozan engi*, there were thirty lodgings for pilgrims at Kasagi, and at one time or another five hundred ascetics—manifestations of Miroku or Kannon—had practiced austerities at the mountain. The text suggests that the ascetics spent their time meditating on such potent Buddhist icons as the Lotus sūtra and images of buddhas in the esoteric pantheon and dodging the evil represented by the mountain's demon, a hungry black serpent one hundred feet in length that was "overjoyed whenever it saw a person."

Pilgrimages to sacred mountains were popular at the Heian court, and Kasagi, like its neighbor Mt. Kinpu, attracted its share of aristocratic notice. The tenth-century court lady Sei Shōnagon mentions Kasagidera in a list of temples in her famous *Pillow Book* (1977, 2:103), and in 1118 Fujiwara Munetada recorded a visit to the temple in his diary *Chūyūki* (1915–1916, 5:82 [1118/9/27]). Munetada and his companions dedicated sūtras before the image of Miroku, praying for the souls of their ancestors and the late emperor. Other distinguished pilgrims to Kasagidera were Fujiwara Yorimichi, regent to the throne, who visited during the Manju era (1024–1027), and Retired Emperor Go Shirakawa, who came in the Angen era (1175–1176) (Sōshō 1960:242).

Jōkei and the Kasagidera Kanjin Campaign

Despite such attention, the temple seems to have been poorly endowed. It must have held some land, but the earliest mention of Kasagidera holdings that I have found is in 1174, in a reference to a lawsuit over hemp fields of unspecified dimensions in an unspecified location (Takeuchi 1963–1976, 10:174 [supp. doc. 121]). The temple was small and probably did not have many monks to support, but revenue for services and construction projects had to come from somewhere. Like other temples of its type, Kasagidera sought that revenue through a kanjin campaign, which was initiated in 1182.

The campaign began as a limited effort, probably supervised by the handful of monks who lived at the temple. The names of three monks besides Jōkei appear on the kanjin requests: Shinchō, Nyokyō, and Kanshun. We know little about them, except that Shinchō also signed a kanjin appeal in 1201 for Gangōji (Sōshō 1960:246–247). If they actually wrote the kanjin requests—and this has been called into question—they were learned men, well versed in Buddhist lore and doctrine, and capable of expressing their ideas in classical Chinese. The three men seem to have been resident monks at the temple rather than muen hijiri who had hired themselves out for temporary kanjin work. However, if the campaign followed standard patterns, some of the legwork must have been performed by muen hijiri, perhaps those who practiced ascetic regimens on the mountain.

At first it seems that a modest band of twelve, led by Nyokyō himself, collected gifts and recorded each donor's name in a rollbook. Even though donations were to be sought from "supporters both near and far" (Sōshō 1960:235), the limited goals of the early campaign suggest that it was conducted fairly close to home. The fact that written appeals were issued indicates careful planning and coordination, however, and Jōkei's participation—which began at least in 1192 but possibly before—lent the campaign prestige and resulted in large donations. Finally, at the end of the campaign, the court was asked to sanction the most ambitious project, the rebuilding of the Raidō (worship hall). Such factors differentiate the campaign from small-scale efforts conducted by muen hijiri.

Although the campaign as a whole resulted in a complete renovation of the old temple, the objectives of each request were quite specific. The effort began in 1182 with a search for offerings to support religious ceremonies described simply as nenbutsu services. In the next year funds were sought for rites in which monks would chant the Hachimyō darani sūtra and contemplate Miroku (Sōshō 1960:236, 234).[3] (Both efforts are described in later kanjin requests.) The earliest kanjin requests, dated 1185, specify offerings of rice to feed the monks performing these services. In 1188 monks sought donations to construct a small pagoda and to make a sandalwood image of Miroku to be placed inside it.

The campaign might have remained a modest one had it not been for Jōkei, a monk of great talent who abandoned a successful ascent through the monastic hierarchy to live in retreat at the mountain temple. Jōkei was born in 1155, the grandson of the counselor of state Shinzei (Fujiwara Michinori), whose involvement in the Heiji uprising cost him his life in 1159.[4] Jōkei was sent to Nara in 1162, and three years later, at the age of ten, he took Buddhist orders. The details of his early monastic life are not clear, but it is likely that he studied Hossō doctrine under his uncle, Kakuken of Kōfukuji. It is not known when Jōkei developed his interest in restoring Buddhism's framework—its tenets, monastic precepts, images, and buildings. But it appears that throughout his life as a monk he involved himself enthusiastically in the work of restoration, both spiritual and physical, beginning with efforts to revive the precepts at Kōfukuji and culminating in kanjin campaigns at Kōfukuji as well as at Kasagidera (Yoshida 1972:200; Yasuda 1983:69).

Jōkei's interest in Kasagidera dates from 1182, when he vowed to copy the Lotus sūtra and dedicate it at the temple, a project that took him eleven years to complete (Yoshida 1972: 182). He may have been involved in the temple's kanjin campaign almost from its inception; perhaps he is the "certain holy man" who had helped to plan the campaign in 1183, according to one of the kanjin requests (Sōshō 1960:234; Kamata and Tanaka 1971:

463). It may even have been Jōkei who wrote the kanjin requests signed by Shinchō, Nyokyō, and Kanshun (Kamata and Tanaka 1971:463; Tomimura 1977:194), though there seems to be no particular reason why he should not have signed them himself. While still at Kōfukuji, Jōkei attracted the attention of leading figures at the capital in Kyōto. An accomplished orator, he was asked to perform the eight lectures on the Lotus sūtra at Hōjōji in 1191 at the service on the anniversary of the death of the eldest son of Kujō Kanezane, regent to the throne and the most powerful civilian aristocrat in the nation. When the regent visited Nara later that year to survey the progress of reconstruction at Kōfukuji, Jōkei presided over the reading of sūtras at the temple's Nanendō.

In 1192 Jōkei decided to move to Kasagidera, and over Kanezane's opposition he did so in the fall of the next year. In explaining why he wished to retreat to the mountain temple, Jōkei cited a vow he had made to the Daimyōjin (kami) of Kasuga shrine, in which he announced a desire to be reborn in Miroku's Tosotsu heaven. Thus one reason Jōkei chose Kasagidera was his devotion to Miroku, the temple's focus of worship. In the isolation of the mountain, moreover, he must have found a peaceful world suited to study and the keeping of the clerical precepts. Another motivation for withdrawal may have been his concern with corruption at Kōfukuji as well as the danger of too much involvement in politics—a conclusion he may have drawn from his grandfather's unfortunate fate.

In retreating to Kasagidera, Jōkei was following a time-honored pattern of withdrawal from ordinary monastic affairs, ostensibly in favor of study, meditation, and concerted effort to follow the Buddhist path. This pattern suggests the extent to which important temples, once a means of abandoning the world, had become themselves "the world." Jōkei's withdrawal was partial at best, and he maintained contacts with those in high political office; from his mountain retreat, moreover, he helped to shape the Nara revival by promoting central elements in its outreach to lay believers: the veneration of relics, faith in the Lotus sūtra, and the worship of Miroku.

Two projects at Kasagidera seem to have been close to Jōkei's heart. These were the restoration of the eight lectures on the Lotus sūtra, the ceremony that had won him fame in Kyōto, and a dedication service for relics of the Buddha. Jōkei personally signed kanjin requests for these projects, something he did not even do for the reconstruction of the Raidō, the major undertaking in terms of expense.

Support for biannual lectures was sought first in 1193 and again in 1196. According to the written requests issued on these occasions, the lectures were an ancient tradition at the temple, initiated in 794. When the temple found itself short of materials, however, it could not continue with the ceremonies. The requests lament the monks' torn clothes and broken bowls, and the temple's missing flags and canopies (Sōshō 1960:237–240).

In the two kanjin requests that he signed in 1196, Jōkei outlined his intentions to expand the temple's services and its physical framework (Sōshō 1960:238–240). He planned to construct a thirteen-tiered pagoda which would contain copies of the three-part Mahayana sūtra (the Lotus, Dai Hannya, and Shinjikan sūtras), relics of the Buddha, and images of the bodhisattva Monju and the four heavenly kings. Sixteen monks would be chosen to conduct the initial services, a recitation in abbreviated fashion of the Lotus sūtra; recitations of the other two sūtras would be added later. In addition, Jōkei planned a thousand-day kuyō (dedication service) for the relics, issuing a kanjin request that sought ten bowls of rice a day for the duration of the service.

It is no surprise that Jōkei concentrated his efforts on the Lotus sūtra and relics, since both were objects of widespread veneration in the late Heian and Kamakura periods. Ideas from the Lotus sūtra informed poetry and painting as well as religious worship, and popular legends told of oxen or serpents reborn as humans through the sūtra's miraculous power.[5] In addition, the Lotus sūtra was often buried in anticipation of the advent of Miroku as the next Buddha. As for relics—fragments believed to be Shakyamuni Buddha's ashes—they were an apt expression of the central urge of the Nara revival, to return to the purity of the Buddha's time. Both the Lotus sūtra and relics had meaning for the lay believer: the teachings of the sūtra opened the way for all to attain buddhahood, and relics provided a tangible, physical reminder of the founder of Buddhism. Thus both were useful tools to link the Nara revival with potential lay supporters.

The major building project at Kasagidera was the reconstruction of the Raidō, the hall from which the Miroku image was worshiped. According to one of the kanjin requests issued in 1203, the old building was too small to hold the people that the temple's revival had attracted: "When monks and laity throng to this garden of majestic Buddhist ceremonies, there is no room to accommodate them all, and many are so far away that they cannot see or hear" (Sōshō 1960:240). Moreover, worshipers inside the old Raidō could not see the entire image, probably because it was too large and too close to the building to permit a full view. The project was either too expensive or too important to rely entirely on public goodwill; the court was asked to recognize the project by granting the temple a high official rank, thus making it easier to appeal for donations.

The kanjin campaign seems to have been successful. The Raidō was completed in 1204, with gifts including gold dust from the shōgun Minamoto Sanetomo (Hayakawa 1923, 2:9 [1204/4/ 10]). In remarks written for the building's dedication, Jōkei thanked donors for help with the construction of a sūtra library and a pagoda (Sōshō 1960:232). Moreover, documents indicate that at the end of the campaign Kasagidera held rights to several parcels of land (Takeuchi 1971–1991, 2:216–218, 349–352 [docs. 902, 1063, 1064], 3:15–16 [doc. 1204]). It seems likely that some or all of these were donations to the kanjin effort. One holding was Hannya manor in Iga province, consisting of three *chō* eight *tan* (roughly 9.4 acres) of paddy and dry fields donated by a local landholder. Rights to this land, including tax exemptions and immunity from entry by provincial officals, were confirmed in 1199 by the retired emperor's office. Kasagidera also had rights to an unspecified amount of land in Yamashiro province, a gift of Retired Emperor Go Shirakawa, and to Sugimoto manor in Yamato province, cited in a document of 1201 as a gift of Hachijō In (1136–1211), daughter of Emperor Toba.[6]

Welcome as such gifts were, they were not the sole aim of the campaign, as I will argue later in this chapter. Rather, the Kasagidera monks sought and expected to receive small gifts. Like kanjin solicitors from other temples, they sought help from every quarter, mustering the blessings of elites and the sanction of precedent to attract gifts from everyone. In seeking alms, moreover, kanjin solicitors preached to potential donors. What they told people–

about images, temples, miracles, and the value of charity–helped to produce vital and compelling forms of religion that involved all segments of the population.

Telling Kasagidera's Story in the Kanjin Requests

The search for donations required that kanjin hijiri appeal directly to potential converts in terms they could accept and understand. They had not only to expound simplified Buddhist teachings, but also to connect these teachings with existing popular concepts. Rather than asking people to discard their old religious beliefs and practices, hijiri recast these elements and combined them with Buddhist teachings, enabling ordinary people to accept a religious system that otherwise would have seemed both foreign and intellectually formidable.

For most people in twelfth-century Japan, religion was firmly grounded in things they could touch and see. The kami venerated from prehistoric times were thought to inhabit particular physical locations such as great trees or mountains, and often there was no clear distinction between the kami and its habitat. In other words, a sacred place could be a kami in itself. In theory Buddhism took a far more complex view of physical phenomena, but in practice special importance was given to the physical components of a temple, including its setting, its buildings, and its sculpture and paintings. These elements became part of the temple's "story," a weave of legend, fantasy, hyperbole, and factual records. The historical truth of all these elements is not at issue, since the importance of the story lay not in its veracity, but in its ability to generate an image of the temple that motivated hijiri to devote themselves to its causes and lay believers to offer their support.

Medieval kanjin hijiri frequently told their temples' stories in attempt to open the pockets of potential givers. In their kanjin requests, temples often claimed miraculous origins and connections with exalted figures of both past and present. It was a rare temple that did not cite imperial visits, miraculous origins, or connections with saints of Buddhist history such as Shōtoku Taishi, Gyōki, or En no Gyōja.

In his study of the thirteenth-century setsuwa collection *Hasedera Kannon genki,* Nagai Yoshinori argues that its tales were composed, embellished, and circulated by kanjin hijiri (1953:20–22).

According to Nagai, hijiri attracted donors by adding concrete details to accounts that in earlier versions had been vague and sketchy. Nagai also points out that many miracle tales appear in different collections in almost identical form, the only difference being the name of the temple where the miracle occurred. This fact suggests that hijiri used the tales as raw material for kanjin purposes. For example, the founding legend of Chōkyūji, a Yamato temple that issued a kanjin request in 1208, closely resembles that of Kasagidera. When Son'amidabutsu sought donations to rebuild Chōkyūji, he recounted the tale of the courtier Fujiwara Yoshitsugu (726–777), caught in a tight spot one day when he was out on a hunting expedition. Yoshitsugu prayed to the bodhisattva Kannon for assistance, promising to carve an image and build a temple at the site. Returning later, he used his bow to carve an image of Kannon, which he worshiped night and day. Sometime afterward he took scraps from the log used to make the famous Hasedera Kannon and carved a smaller image of the bodhisattva, enshrining it in a chapel he had built there and thereby founding the temple (Takeuchi 1971–1991, 3:370 [doc. 1771]).

Another type of Buddhist literature that may have been used in kanjin appeals was the engi, the form of the temple's story sanctioned by the institution. In addition to factual material such as lists of buildings, images, and ceremonies, engi typically include miracle tales centered on the temple's main image and exaggerate connections with the imperial family or famous religious figures. In his discussion of this genre, Sakurai Tokutarō suggests an evangelistic purpose for such passages (Sakurai, Hagiwara, and Miyata 1975:467, 472). He points out that in the Kamakura period engi served as guidebooks for pilgrims visiting famous Nara temples. Illustrated texts *(emaki)* were displayed at festivals and other occasions when large numbers of people gathered. Surely alms were collected on these occasions. Like setsuwa, engi probably supplied material for kanjin hijiri and may have been embellished by them as well.

Kasagidera engi was not recorded until the sixteenth century, but the temple's story had begun to take shape by the end of the twelfth century, when Kasagidera launched its kanjin campaign and issued written requests (*Kasagidera engi* 1913:87–111). Kasagidera's story—the legends and miracles that made it a holy place—was an important component of the kanjin appeals, since it helped to explain why people should favor the temple and to make concrete the spiritual benefits promised to potential donors.

The veneration of Miroku lay at the heart of Kasagidera's story and served as an appropriate symbol for constructing the temple's future through reconstructing its past. As Shakyamuni's successor and image, Miroku was an apt focus for those who not only yearned for original Buddhism but also sought a salvationist faith to answer the needs of a new age. Portrayed as a bodhisattva in the present as well as a buddha for the future, Miroku symbolized the promise of salvation for both the individual and the entire world.[7] The bodhisattva Miroku was thought to welcome the faithful to his Tosotsu heaven after death, just as Amida welcomed believers to his Pure Land. On achieving buddhahood some billions of years in the future, Miroku would descend to earth to preach, enlightening all those reborn there at that fortunate time. Belief in Miroku as either a bodhisattva or a buddha fulfilled the individual's longing for personal salvation after death. In addition, the prediction of Miroku's advent modified the dread of mappō, since the coming of a new buddha assured the end of bad times, an eventual upturn in the cosmic cycle.

Kasagidera's kanjin requests draw on both aspects of Miroku-as-savior, coloring the promise of salvation with the legend of the supernatural origin of the Miroku image, its connection to an imperial prince, and the miracles and power attributed to it. The image exalted the temple, kanjin hijiri said, winning it patrons and making it rival India's holy places (Sōshō 1960:238, 240). Donations to Miroku's "incomparable place of miracles" would result in appropriate rewards: "Those of us who sympathize with the temple and support it with alms will be reborn together in the Chisoku [Tosotsu] heaven and assemble before Jison [Miroku]. On the day of his advent we will descend to earth along with him" (Sōshō 1960:234–235). Thus gift and ultimate result were defined concretely and were organically linked.

The kanjin appeals also emphasized the temple's connections with important people and institutions. According to tales recounted in detail in *Kasagidera engi* and cited in the kanjin requests, the eighth-century prelate Rōben made a pilgrimage to Kasagi during his search for materials for the construction of Tōdaiji, and his disciple Jitchū performed austerities at Kasagidera that were rewarded with a vision of the Tosotsu heaven—or perhaps it was a miraculous visit (Sōshō 1960:241). The brief references to these episodes in the kanjin appeals suggest that these important elements of the temple's story were already well known to potential donors. The kanjin appeals also bragged of the visits of Fujiwara Yorimichi and Go Shirakawa. Such visits, paid by elites that claimed ritual as well as political authority, validated the temple within the politicoreligious system of the Japanese state.

If You Donate Just a Little . . .

From whom did the Kasagidera monks seek donations? Nyokyō and Shinchō said that they would first appeal to longtime supporters, but if contributions were insufficient, other donors would be sought. Both the 1193 request and Jōkei's request of 1196 asked for donations from lay supporters. This evidence suggests that there was already a network of support on which the temple could rely but that contributions from others would have to be found as well.

What of the donors' wealth and social status? We know that the shōgun and perhaps a retired emperor and an imperial princess gave large contributions to the Kasagidera campaign. Support from exalted figures was sometimes explicitly sought. In 1196, for example, Jōkei vowed to dedicate the eight lectures on the Lotus sūtra to the grand shrine at Ise. Since the shrine's chief kami was Amaterasu, claimed as ancestor by the imperial family, the vow was probably an attempt to attract significant donations from the court. The request for high court rank for the temple in conjunction with the rebuilding of the Raidō may perhaps be seen in the same light.

Although the documents contain no direct information concerning donors' status, they do provide some clues, albeit contradictory ones. Written in Chinese characters and full of difficult terms and concepts, the kanjin requests were impossible for anyone but the well educated to read. But traveling hijiri (such as the twelve men mentioned in the Kasagidera kanjin requests) may have read them aloud to potential donors or used them as texts from which appropriate exhortations could be taken. Setsuwa collections, which probably furnished material for popular evangelists' sermons (Ury 1979:2), were also sometimes written in Chinese and sometimes contained terminology as abstruse as that of the kanjin requests. An example is the eleventh-century collection *Hokke genki* (Inoue and Ōsone 1974:44–219; Dykstra 1983). Despite difficulties and obscurities throughout the tales, their major theme—devotion to the Lotus sūtra—was simple enough to understand. Nor would even simple people have misunderstood the basic premises of the kanjin requests: the founding miracle of the temple, its sacredness to Miroku, and the disproportionate reward for a small donation.

The emphasis on small donations was common to kanjin campaigns. Hijiri often asked for specks of dust, twigs, small tools, or half a penny, in phrasing reminiscent of the words of Shōmu when seeking donations to construct Tōdaiji in the eighth century. Such requests were made by the hijiri who sought donations to Chinkōji in 1075, to Tōdaiji in 1181, and to Daianji in 1204 (Takeuchi 1963–1976, 3:1122–1125 [doc. 1110]; *Tōdaiji zoku yōroku* 1907:200; Takeuchi 1971–1991, 3:140 [doc. 1449]). The Kasagidera appeals also specify suitable small donations. Unlike dust and twigs, these donations were of practical value and were probably both expected and welcome. Shinchō said that because the monks' begging bowls had been broken, they would like to have new ones cast. Kanshun requested a small contribution such as a begging bowl or a tenth of a *monme* (thirty-five to forty grams of an unspecified material, possibly gold dust); alms could be given according to the ability of the donor. Both Nyokyō and Shinchō asked for a small gift of one *shō* (a little under two quarts) of rice per month for as long as the donor was able to give. Itō Kazuhiko argues that the people most likely to respond to Shinchō's request of one shō per month for, say, a year were shōen officials or small holders (1980:318). The amount of one shō, which appears in kanjin documents of other temples, appears to have been a standard donation; it was considered enough to feed one monk for a day (Collcutt 1981:221).

Since the Kasagidera requests do not explicitly address the question of audience, perhaps evidence from another kanjin effort can shed some light on the matter. A donation rollbook for Katsuragawa Myōōin in Ōmi province records the kanjin efforts of a single day in 1272 (Takeuchi 1971–1991, 15:23 [doc. 11110]). The rollbook lists fifty-six gifts of cash and rice, including five hundred *mon* (a unit of coinage) from the jitō, two hundred mon from the *kumon* (a shōen official), and one hundred mon from another kumon. The record does not specify their estate, but perhaps they were all officials of the nearby Katsuragawa manor. Most of the gifts were in rice. Of the thirty-one people who gave one shō apiece, most are listed with neither office nor surname, suggesting that they were at best small holders.

The Kasagidera monks, in requesting small gifts such as one shō, a tenth of a monme, or a begging bowl, probably aimed their campaign at a broad range of potential donors, beginning with local notables and including small holders like the ones who gave to Myōōin. Of course, the monks hoped to attract substantial contributions (thus they asked givers to donate every month), but they were realistic enough to accept small, one-time-only gifts. Indeed, the emphasis on small gifts in the requests of other temples suggests that we can draw similar conclusions about kanjin campaigns in general. Gifts were sought from anyone who could give even a tiny amount, which probably meant all segments of society except the destitute.

Why Hold a Kanjin Campaign?

Why did the Kasagidera monks choose to conduct a broad-based kanjin campaign and to continue it for over twenty years? The most obvious answer is that the temple was in need. Like most religious institutions of the time, it depended on income from agricultural land. Competition for land rights was stiff, and Kasagidera was not a large or influential temple. Thus when funds were needed to reconstruct buildings, Kasagidera may have found itself in the same position Daianji was in when in 1204 it conducted a kanjin campaign because it could not live on the income from its shōen (Takeuchi 1971–1991, 3:140 [doc. 1449]). But there is also evidence that by 1201 the temple was hardly in dire straits. In that year Jōkei was able to commend five *koku* (about twenty-five bushels) of rice from Hannya manor and the produce of one chō in Sugimoto manor as votive offerings to Kasuga shrine (Takeuchi 1971–1991, 3:15–16 [doc. 1204]). If the temple was not in immediate need, however, why was the campaign continued vigorously for two or three more years?

A plausible explanation rests on long-term economic considerations. Joan R. Piggott has pointed out that as early as the 1180s and 1190s, even Tōdaiji found it increasingly difficult to maintain a steady flow of revenue from shōen to monastery (1982:74–76). The problem was that real control of shōen income was falling into local hands. By the mid-thirteenth century, large institutions such as Tōdaiji began to seek alternatives, such as the collection of tolls at barriers. For smaller temples such as Kasagidera, the crisis may have come earlier and been more acute. During the period of the kanjin campaign, in fact, Kasagidera became involved in a dispute over rights to Hannya manor. When provincial officials attempted to levy taxes on the fields, Kasagidera asked the retired emperor's office to intervene. An edict issued in 1199 confirmed the temple's rights, declaring that Hannya manor was Kasagidera's territory *(ryō)* in perpetuity (Takeuchi 1971–1991, 2:349–352 [docs. 1063, 1064]). In addition to its holdings in other provinces, the temple's own compound was subject to violation. A petition to the court dated 1197 complained that cultivators from a neighboring manor had cleared land and planted crops on temple precincts without authorization (Takeuchi 1971–1991, 2:216–218 [doc. 902]).

Incidents such as these may help to explain the increasing frequency and regularity of kanjin efforts in the Kamakura period, involving not only small institutions such as Kasagidera but also larger ones such as Kōfukuji, and Kongōbuji on Mt. Kōya. Monks may have perceived the entire economic foundation of Buddhist monasteries as insecure. In short, the times must have seemed ripe for new methods and new supporters, especially local warriors and small holders, the backbone of rural society. Attempts to exploit local wealth and power made even more sense than before.

But economics alone cannot explain why temples undertook kanjin campaigns. The amounts collected were too small and the effort too great and too prone to failure. Throughout the Kamakura period, temples complained of shortfalls or other hindrances to kanjin campaigns, and some found it more advantageous to seek government help in the form of new taxes. Others, however, continued to depend on the populace at large, perhaps because a broad-based campaign had certain advantages from a purely religious perspective. In the days of early Indian Buddhism—seen by the Nara revivalist clergy as a golden age—monks had sustained themselves by begging from householders. The kanjin solicitors may have seen themselves in a similar light, as alms seekers who were helping to restore Shakyamuni's past and to construct Miroku's future. Another possibility lies in the desire of the Nara-revival monks to meet the challenge of Hōnen's teachings. In the Kōfukuji petition of 1205, written at Kasagidera just after the successful culmination of the kanjin campaign, Jōkei attacked Hōnen's central argument, that reciting the Amida nenbutsu was the only efficacious means to salvation (Kamata and Tanaka 1971:31–42; Morrell 1983:20–38). This argument, which condemned all other religious activities as useless, was particularly dangerous to Jōkei and others like him, since it denied the value of practices on which they had staked their spiritual lives.

The petition lists nine "errors" committed by Hōnen.[8] The first one, the error of establishing a new sect, is couched in conservative terms, and Hōnen is accused of hubris for daring to liken himself to Saichō and Kūkai, founders of the Japanese Tendai and Shingon schools. Next Jōkei complains about a new Pure Land mandala, criticizing its pictorial suggestion that only Pure Land adherents would bathe in Amida's light: ". . . it is unreasonable to claim that if a person, in his single-minded practice of other good actions, were never to call upon Amida, he would thereby be excluded from the rays which truly embrace all" (Morrell 1983: 21). Jōkei also criticizes Hōnen for slighting the historical Buddha and vilifying his followers, for rejecting good deeds and religious practices other than the nenbutsu, for neglecting the kami, and for causing disorder in the nation. In other words, the crux of Jōkei's argument is directed against Hōnen's intolerance of other practices, an attitude seen as having disastrous consequences for society as a whole.

When considered in the light of the efforts of Jōkei and others to reform their own schools, Hōnen's viewpoint must have seemed particularly galling. Not only did it condemn their work as useless, it also challenged the concept of hōben that justified religious eclecticism and governed the transmission of Buddhist teachings to lay believers. According to the Kōfukuji petition, the recital of the nenbutsu without meditating or concentrating on the Buddha —the practice recommended by Hōnen—might be "good enough for certain individuals in a worldly state of mind" (Morrell 1983:30), but other practices were more suitable for those of higher spiritual attainments. The converse—that simple methods

of achieving salvation were available to those in need of them—
was emphasized time and time again in the kanjin requests. In
them, Miroku, like Amida, is presented as a compassionate savior
whose grace is available to all, since he had vowed, "I will not
even discard those who do not think of me. How much less so
those who yearn for me!" (Sōshō 1960:236).

Even so, there was an important difference between Hōnen's
Pure Land teachings and the salvationism propounded by the
Nara monks. In the Pure Land scheme, salvation depended only
on a believer's faith and Amida Buddha's grace. The Nara
monks, however, argued that salvation required positive action by
the believer. Yet this action did not have to be arduous or costly.
The argument that small donations would produce great rewards
was the nucleus of the Kasagidera requests. When Jōkei wrote:
"The dedication of a small offering shall without fail enable you to
see the Buddha, hear his teachings, aim at enlightenment, and fulfill that aim" (Sōshō 1960:238), he was claiming that a small gift
would initiate a sequence of inevitable events—each involving the
giver's will and effort—that would eventually result in buddhahood. A good deed such as the construction of a pagoda might be
performed collectively, and merit sufficient for salvation would
accrue to each participant. Thus the construction of monastery
buildings and the support of Buddhist services was not the province of the wealthy alone.

Requests for small contributions, moreover, can be seen not
only as an attempt to attract the impecunious but also as an effort
to cut to size the moral requirements for salvation. There are
many examples in Kasagidera's kanjin requests: "If you give alms
to living beings even once, you still form the good karma to meet
with Miroku" (Sōshō 1960:235). "Even those who sink into the
miserable worlds of hell, hungry ghosts, or beasts can rely on the
encounter with Miroku at his advent" (Sōshō 1960:241), just as
even the wicked, in Hōnen's teachings, might rely on Amida. A
similar theme was repeated by Jōkei in his treatise Shin'yōshō, written in 1212 near the end of his life. He argued that, in the age of
mappō, those who "keep the precepts or break the precepts, hold
the precepts or lack the precepts" would attain salvation at the
time of Miroku's advent (Takakusu and Watanabe 1924–1932,
71:58 [no. 2311]).

In their efforts to put salvation within anyone's reach, the

Kasagidera monks occupied the mainstream of Kamakura Buddhism. Certainly they were motivated in part by economic needs. We might view kanjin cynically as an attempt to prosper by coopting the methods that had attracted followers to Hōnen. But, in fact, the Kasagidera efforts and the Nara school revival sprang from the same combination of reaction to social and political upheaval and maturing comprehension of Buddhist teachings that had produced Hōnen's movement. Like Hōnen, monks of the kenmitsu schools had assessed their own times and declared them the age of mappō; like Hōnen, these monks sought a proper spiritual response to the "decadence" of the age; and like Hōnen, they chose to respond in a way that offered comfort to large numbers of people. If economic pressure made it necessary for temples to seek new donors, the monks' own spiritual goals made it necessary for them to seek new converts.

The efforts of monks such as Jōkei and others who conducted kanjin campaigns had far more influence on subsequent developments in Buddhism than is generally recognized. Despite Hōnen's insistence that the nenbutsu alone was sufficient for salvation, lay believers did not discard other practices. They pooled their resources to have images made, temples repaired, and services recited for the dead, and they embarked on pilgrimages to temples and shrines. It was as if people took to heart the declaration of religious eclecticism made by Jōkei in *Shin'yōshō:* "In the latter days, there are Amida and Miroku for buddhas, the Lotus and Hannya for sūtras, the nenbutsu and reading the sūtras for religious activities, and for places to be reborn there are the Gokuraku paradise [of Amida] and the Tosotsu heaven" (Kamata and Tanaka 1971: 468; Takakusu and Watanabe 1924–1932, 71:62 [no. 2311]).

The eclecticism of the older Buddhist schools was far more than just a tolerant outlook; it was the very pillar that supported outreach to lay believers, whether through kanjin or other means. Clerics such as Jōkei tried to revive monastic Buddhism by adhering strictly to the precepts, in hopes of reproducing the religious purity that they attributed to Shakyamuni's Buddhism. At the same time they stressed paths to salvation that were simple to comprehend and easy to follow, thus—like Hōnen—making Buddhism accessible to lay believers. These two aspects of the Nara revival seem contradictory, but they were organically connected.

Early in this chapter I suggested that the Nara revival might fit Victor Turner's definition of a revivalist movement that aimed to recreate the communitas of the religion in its earliest days. Seen from two different perspectives—that of the monk and that of the lay believer—the Nara revival seems to have had this aim. On the one hand, monks such as Jōkei formed special communities bound by their observance of the precepts. On the other hand, the actions of Jōkei and others like him manifested the belief that everyone had the buddha-nature and that, therefore, the Buddhist message must be extended to everyone. The entire reconstruction effort at Kasagidera—the crafting of the temple's story, the search for donors from various social levels, and the emphasis on collective action—can be seen as efforts to fulfill this goal.

The creation of communities of willing donors also had implications for society at large: these communities could be used by their members as bases for political action or manipulated by holders or seekers of power. Moreover, the very idea of public, voluntary support for temples also produced political capital for the temples themselves and for their prominent lay patrons. When important political figures such as the retired emperor or the shōgun donated to kanjin campaigns and convinced others to do likewise, they were enhancing their own prestige and authority and thus their political control. The donations to Kasagidera from dignitaries such as Go Shirakawa should probably be seen in this light.

The retired emperor was always eager to advance his own political causes through patronizing temples. His most significant opportunity came when a fire in 1180 destroyed Japan's most splendid monastery, the imperial temple Tōdaiji. The next chapter will tell how Go Shirakawa and later, the shōgun, manipulated Tōdaiji's misfortune to their own advantage, and how their actions benefited Tōdaiji and broadened the use of kanjin methods.

Four

HALF A PENNY OR A SCRAP OF WOOD: CHŌGEN AND THE CAMPAIGN FOR TŌDAIJI

In the last month of the fourth year of Jishō (1180), the great Nara temple Tōdaiji was set aflame by the armies of the Taira.[1] The conflagration, which destroyed not only Tōdaiji but its neighbor temple Kōfukuji and other monuments of Nara Buddhism, was a prelude to the Genpei war between the Taira and their rivals the Minamoto.

Major buildings of Tōdaiji were destroyed or severely damaged, including the Daibutsuden and the eighth-century image of Roshana Buddha within. The initial stages of the project to reconstruct Tōdaiji, begun the next year, were primarily the work of two individuals, Retired Emperor Go Shirakawa and Chōgen, a monk who had spent his early religious life as a wandering hijiri.[2] With Go Shirakawa's encouragement, Chōgen sought financing for the project through a nationwide kanjin campaign.

Complex and costly, the reconstruction of Tōdaiji took many years to accomplish, but the first step, the recasting of the image's head, was finished in 1185, shortly before the victory of the Minamoto. The earliest stage of the project, in short, was completed while the country was still in the throes of civil conflict and in dire economic straits. Moreover, although Kōfukuji had been destroyed at the same time, it never became the object of a similar nationwide restoration effort. Tōdaiji had special claims to national attention: originally constructed by Emperor Shōmu as both a symbol of imperial power and a mechanism for the exercise of that power, it could not be left in ruins. The restoration, moreover, was especially important for a monarchy buffeted by war and by challenges to its prerogatives by an upstart warrior class, and for a civilian aristocracy that depended on the institution of the monarchy for its political power.

The rebuilding of Tōdaiji had significant implications both for the exercise of political power and for the development of Buddhism's appeal for all social classes. Secular power formation and religious revival converged to produce a community of believers that cooperated to rebuild the temple with any means at their disposal.

The use of a kanjin campaign to raise revenue for Tōdaiji's restoration was intended by Go Shirakawa to bolster the power and authority of the throne. The campaign was reminiscent of Gyōki's efforts when the temple was founded in the mid-eighth century, when the monarchy was at the height of its political power. Moreover, in requesting the voluntary help of all the people to rebuild a monument to imperial glory, the throne involved the public in an integrated project that transcended the divisions of early medieval society. In effect, the rebuilding of Tōdaiji—and the way in which revenue was sought for the project—was meant to strengthen the throne's claim to jurisdiction over all Japan, in contrast to the more limited claims of the *bushi* (warrior) houses involved in the Genpei war. Ironically, the project also served the interests of Minamoto Yoritomo (1147–1199), chief of the victorious bushi faction who eventually became the shōgun. Through supporting the Tōdaiji reconstruction, Yoritomo also sought legitimation for his power, but the fact that his power was based on military force dictated differences in the way that legitimation was pursued. The practical problems of reconstruction required his help, even though his participation in the project ultimately advanced his own cause at the expense of Go Shirakawa's; thus the two cooperated, each for reasons of his own.

The pivotal role in harnessing political ambition to religious revival was played by Chōgen, a man who turned his status as a marginal hijiri into a position of power and influence, and transformed a basically elite undertaking—the reconstruction of a state temple—into an opportunity to spread a popular faith. The alliance between Chōgen and Go Shirakawa—one at the apex of the social structure, the other at its margins—created at least the perception that the Tōdaiji campaign was supported by the entire nation, the community as a whole. Chōgen employed this percep-

tion to create a solid community of believers that supported not
only the Tōdaiji effort but his other projects as well, using kanjin
campaigns and the temples built through them to spread the belief
in Amida and the Pure Land among people of various social
classes.

The Tōdaiji campaign's nationwide scope and its links to
throne and shōgun made it unusual among kanjin campaigns, but
the aims of its exalted sponsors were similar to the aims of lesser
political authorities who appropriated kanjin means throughout
the Kamakura period, and the methods used by Chōgen were
adopted by other temples conducting kanjin efforts on a smaller
scale. Thus the Tōdaiji campaign can help to shed light on the
ways in which temples, through kanjin, used and were used by
political authorities to enhance the power of both.

Tōdaiji and the Throne

By the twelfth century, neither Tōdaiji nor the throne entirely fulfilled Shōmu's conception of them as powerful centers of, respec-
tively, the state religious system and the state itself. In 822, when
the court permitted monks to be ordained at the Tendai center at
Mt. Hiei, Tōdaiji's earlier monopoly over entry into the clergy
was broken. Perhaps even more important was the dissolution of
the entire system of state control over Buddhism in the Heian
period: scores of unofficial temples were founded, unauthorized
monks moved freely among the people, and the framework of official Buddhism was severely weakened. Tōdaiji remained an
important temple and became a powerful landholder and political
force, but it was no longer the center of an integrated structure. As
for the throne, it was deprived of much of its income by tax
exemptions granted to the shōen, and the regnant emperors were
weakened and manipulated first by their maternal (Fujiwara) relatives and then by abdicated emperors who exercised power behind
the scenes. Nonetheless, the throne retained its institutional primacy as the ultimate source of official appointments and the confirmation of land rights.

In 1180, however, that primacy must have seemed in danger
from the expanding power of the bushi clans. The head of the
Taira, Kiyomori, had been ensconced in Kyōto since 1159. His
attempt to dominate the throne, although patterned after Fuji-

wara methods, was much more heavy-handed than theirs had ever been: Kiyomori went so far as to place Retired Emperor Go Shira-kawa under house arrest at one point and even moved the capital briefly to his own power base at Fukuhara along the Inland Sea. In eastern Japan, Minamoto Yoritomo was expanding his hege-mony over the area, perhaps even planning to establish an inde-pendent rebel state (Hurst 1982:5–6). In short, the throne was at a crisis point in 1180, even before the destruction of Tōdaiji. When Go Shirakawa set out to restore the temple, he was not only attempting to rebuild an important Buddhist institution, he was also restoring a powerful symbol of imperial rule.

Go Shirakawa and the Tōdaiji Kanjin Campaign

Go Shirakawa has not fared well in history, nor was he honored in his own time.[3] Minamoto Yoritomo called him "Japan's greatest *tengu* (goblin)," and an oracle circulated during his lifetime evalu-ated him thus: "The retired emperor's character is not sincere; he follows fashion and is inconstant; his heart is not at peace; while such a situation prevails, uprisings will not cease in the realm" (Takeuchi 1978:272). The creators of *Heike monogatari* depicted him as sly and wily, playing one bushi and noble against another, with constant thought of his own advantage. Even his own man Fujiwara Michinori (Shinzei), who conducted the affairs of the In-no-chō (Retired Emperor's Office) until his own death in the Heiji war of 1159, characterized Go Shirakawa as an unenlightened ruler "without parallel in the history of China and Japan" (San-som 1958:267). His alleged inconstancy and manipulativeness, however, can also be seen as pragmatism in defense of the throne's prerogatives.

Although it was thought proper for monarchs to patronize lit-erature and religion, Go Shirakawa was also criticized for exces-sive devotion to both (Takeuchi 1978:267, 273). Because he had been absorbed since his childhood in *imayō*, a form of popular poetry, his father, Retired Emperor Toba, considered him unwor-thy to take the throne, and he became emperor only because there was no other suitable candidate at the time of Emperor Konoe's sudden death in 1155. He retained his interest in imayō through-out his lifetime, collecting the poems—many on Buddhist themes —in the anthology *Ryōjin hishō* and inviting even prostitutes and street minstrels to his palace if they were skilled imayō reciters (Kwon 1986:275). Conservative courtiers must have looked askance at Go Shirakawa's unseemly interest in the lower orders of society; yet it may have helped give him the broad perspective necessary to envision a public campaign to rebuild Tōdaiji that appealed not only to the aristocracy, but to ordinary folk as well.

Go Shirakawa's piety was well known, attracting the attention of such observors as Jien, the Tendai cleric who compiled the history *Gukanshō* in the thirteenth century (Jien 1969:375, Brown and Ishida 1979:105). Critics claimed, however, that his devotion had gone too far, encouraging the depredations of monastic armies and exhausting government resources in the patronage of both Buddhist temples and Shintō shrines (Takeuchi 1978:273–274). Go Shirakawa made thirty-two pilgrimages to Kumano shrine and built several shrines and temples, donating landholdings to support them. His best-known construction project prior to the Tōdaiji rebuilding was Sanjūsangendō (Rengeōin), built in the capital in 1164 and famous for its thousand images of the Thousand-armed Kannon. For this project Go Shirakawa turned to Taira Kiyomori, who defrayed the costs through assessments on Bizen province, where the Taira had extensive holdings (Jien 1969:405, Brown and Ishida 1979:118).

After the Taira victory in the Heiji uprising of 1159, Kiyomori and Go Shirakawa formed an uneasy alliance that lasted for twenty years. At first Kiyomori deferred to the retired emperor (Mass 1974a:127–133)—the financing of Sanjusangendō may be one example—but the bushi leader cleverly established an independent route to power, marrying his daughter to the regnant emperor and becoming, in 1178, the grandfather of the future emperor Antoku. By that time relations between Kiyomori and Go Shirakawa had become quite uncomfortable: neither had forgiven the other for his role in the Shishigatani affair of 1177, in which associates of the retired emperor had plotted against Kiyomori and had been discovered and harshly punished. Kiyomori had even reprimanded Go Shirakawa himself. In 1179, clearly recognizing Kiyomori's maternal connections to the throne as a threat, Go Shirakawa seized Taira land rights and rejected Kiyomori's candidate for high office; Kiyomori responded with a coup d'état in which the retired emperor was placed under house arrest. This act became the pretext for rebellions on the part of the Minamoto, rivals to the Taira. Faced with this agitation, Kiyomori restored Go Shirakawa to his position as the head of the In-no-chō in 1180, but Go Shirakawa remained under the Taira leader's thumb until the latter's death in early 1181.

It is against this background that Go Shirakawa's concern with rebuilding Tōdaiji must be evaluated. A restored Tōdaiji could serve as a monument to the renewed glory of the throne as well as to the perfidy of the Taira (a factor that must also have attracted Minamoto Yoritomo's cooperation somewhat later in the rebuilding process). But where could Go Shirakawa obtain funding for such a massive project?

State support for Tōdaiji, like other important Buddhist institutions, had been provided initially by land allotments and tax revenues from designated sustenance households. When revenue from these sources became unreliable, Tōdaiji increased its efforts to develop shōen, which it could control more directly (Piggott 1982:52–53). For purposes of repair, however, official temples such as Tōdaiji could still lay claim to state funds (Yasuda 1983:66). Thus Tōdaiji had two possible sources to fund its reconstruction project: it could milk its own shōen, and it could receive public assistance through taxes. But the scramble for funding that took place early in 1181 suggests that sufficient revenue could be obtained from neither source.

Although the destruction of Tōdaiji caused much distress in the imperial court, little could be done to repair the damage as long as the government and Go Shirakawa himself were under Kiyomori's control. Moreover, the Taira had forced the confiscation of Tōdaiji estates (Kujō 1908, I, 2:463 [1181/1/8]), thus cutting the temple off from its income. It was not until Kiyomori died in the intercalary second month of 1181 that reconstruction activities could be initiated. Even then Go Shirakawa proceeded cautiously, blaming not the Taira but "bad elements" at Tōdaiji and Kōfukuji for the burning and only tentatively suggesting that the temples' estates be restored (Kujō 1908, I, 2:489 [1181/intercalary 2/20]). Though the holdings were returned shortly,[4] Tōdaiji's financial problems were not solved, as Kujō Kanezane, then minister of the right, affirmed in his diary Gyokuyō.

The only truly contemporary account of the early stages of Tōdaiji's reconstruction is found in this diary, compiled between 1164 and 1200. Although for the most part this information can be accepted as accurate, Kanezane seems to have taken little interest in the detailed planning of the project. Thus the account must be supplemented by other sources that date from somewhat later times, such as Chōgen's *Namuamidabutsu sazenshū* (1934:42-51), written in 1204, and *Hyakurenshō* (Kuroita 1929), a chronicle written in the late Kamakura period. The most detailed and polished account, however, appears in *Tōdaiji zoku yōroku* (1907:195-206), compiled in the late thirteenth century. In this version, the kanjin campaign is described as a purposeful and well-planned effort initiated by determined and pious individuals. In both its tone and some of its factual information, however, this account disagrees at times with Kanezane's. (See Table 1 for a chronology of the first steps of the Tōdaiji reconstruction.)

According to both *Zoku yōroku* and *Gyokuyō,* serious plans for reconstructing Tōdaiji got under way in the third month of 1181. It was then that Fujiwara Yukitaka, an official of Go Shirakawa's In-no-chō and the Kurōdodokoro (Imperial Secretariat), arranged with bronzecasting masters to remake the Daibutsu image. A few days later, when he visited Kanezane on Go Shirakawa's behalf,

Table 1 First Steps in the Reconstruction of Tōdaiji

1180/12/28	Nara temples burned (GY, TZY)
1181/intercalary 2/5	Kiyomori dies (GY)
1181/intercalary 2/20	Yukitaka and Kanezane discuss the possibility of restoring temple shōen (GY)
1181/3/17	Yukitaka contacts casting masters (TZY)
1181/3/21	Yukitaka suggests an imperial request for donations (GY)
1181/4/9	Chōgen volunteers his services (TZY)
1181/6/26	Yukitaka is appointed construction superintendent (GY)
1181/6	Imperial edict orders a kanjin campaign (TZY)
1181/7/14-16	Yukitaka and Kanezane discuss reconstruction financing (GY)
1181/8	Chōgen issues his kanjin appeal (TZY)
1181/10/6	Casting of the Daibutsu is set to begin (GY)
1181/10/9	Chōgen collects donations in Kyōto (GY)

GY: Kujō Kanezane, *Gyokuyō.*
TZY: Kokusho Kankōkai, *Tōdaiji zoku yōroku.*

Yukitaka suggested that an imperial order be issued to chishiki (Buddhist faithful) to implement the casting of the image. The use of the word *chishiki* suggests that there was to be a request for donations, though there is no indication that a nationwide kanjin campaign was considered at this time.

At the end of the sixth month, government officials met to decide on details of the construction project. Yukitaka was appointed construction superintendent, and several other officials of the retired emperor's staff were chosen to assist him (Asai and Asai 1986:16). Following the recommendations of the On'yōryō (Bureau of Divinations), construction work was set to begin in the eighth month. According to an order passed on from Yukitaka to officials of Tōdaiji and of Yamato province, Tōdaiji's sustenance households and shōen would finance the project.

Even so, funding was still a significant problem, and there was considerable danger that the project would not get under way as planned. *Gyokuyō* reports a conversation that took place on 7/13 between Kanezane and Yukitaka, who bore a message from Go Shirakawa (Kujō 1908, I, 2:514–515). The retired emperor complained that the nation had been plagued by a series of calamities —drought, famine, and insurrection—as well as by mysterious events, including a comet and the appearance of two flowers on one stem of a lotus plant, an omen of bad fortune. How, Go Shirakawa asked, can we avoid such misfortunes? Go Shirakawa's complaint was vague, but the destruction of the Nara temples—and the failure of the court to set about immediately to rebuild them— must have been seen as at least one cause of the disasters and bad omens that had befallen the nation. Kanezane's answer implied that this was the case. While sympathizing with the retired emperor's concerns, Kanezane, in his own account the benevolent Confucian minister, refused to consider raising taxes: "Whether we are discussing the restoration of the two temples [Tōdaiji and Kōfukuji] or provisions for warriors of our defending army, if we lay the expenses on the people, it would really be quite a burden for them. Even in good years, these farmers lead hard lives; how much more so when they are dying of starvation!" Kanezane and messengers from Go Shirakawa debated the issue for the next two days without reaching any firm decision.

That autumn, apparently, a decision was made to finance Tōdaiji's reconstruction in part through a kanjin campaign.

Though such campaigns had become quite common by the late twelfth century, they were not the standard means to meet expenses at the temple; as a model for fundraising, Gyōki's effort seemed all but forgotten. Private undertakings rooted in popular religious beliefs, campaigns were more suitable for small and medium-sized temples that obtained their main support from the populace at large than for a great institution such as Tōdaiji, established by imperial order as a religious underpinning for the state. In the difficult times of 1181, however, it must have seemed necessary to seek revenue from every possible source. Even though Tōdaiji's shōen had once more become available, the temple's economic base had been weakening for some time, and the problem was exacerbated by continuing disputes with Kōfukuji over holdings in Yamato province (Asai and Asai 1986:16). In addition, it appears that the traditional mechanism for accomplishing repair work had long since failed the temple: repairs had originally been the responsibility of the bettō, but from late Heian times that office had been filled by Shingon monks who did not live at the temple and sometimes neglected their duties (Nagamura 1981:64). Thus the resident monks at the temple had to look elsewhere, and this necessity prepared the way for the kanjin campaign as an alternate revenue source.

Looking Back to Shōmu

Such explanations are certainly valid, but I think yet another factor should be considered: the desire of the court, especially Go Shirakawa, to use Tōdaiji's reconstruction to enhance the power and prestige of the throne. If a nationwide kanjin campaign were used to collect revenue for the project, it would be a concrete testament to the power of the throne to mobilize people and resources from anywhere in Japan and thus to lay claim as no bushi leader could to jurisdiction over the entire nation.

Calling for a nationwide campaign may have been economically necessary; politically it was a bold step. The Taira still held power in the capital, and Go Shirakawa and Kanezane had to be careful not to offend them. This may be one reason that, in conversations between Kanezane and Go Shirakawa's messengers in the seventh month of 1181, temple reconstruction was joined to two other questions: how to deal with "bad monks"—presumably the ones who had invited the retribution of the Taira—and how to finance the Taira war effort. It seems as if Go Shirakawa and Kanezane were ready to offer the Taira a quid pro quo: do not interfere with our efforts to rebuild Tōdaiji and Kōfukuji, and in exchange we will keep monastic armies under control and provide for your soldiers.

To investigate the kanjin campaign itself and Chōgen's role in implementing it, we must turn to *Tōdaiji zoku yōroku* (1907:195–206). According to this source, Chōgen approached Yukitaka in the fourth month of 1181, explaining that a dream oracle had sent him to visit Tōdaiji, where he had lamented the destruction of the Daibutsu. Yukitaka, recognizing help when he saw it, suggested that an imperial order authorizing a kanjin campaign might be obtained. Such an order was promulgated in the sixth month, and two months later, we are told, Chōgen built six one-wheeled carts, and he and his followers canvassed "the seven circuits and all the provinces," requesting donations through a written appeal. The imperial order and Chōgen's kanjin appeal are reproduced along with a document written in 1185 by Chōgen that corroborates the earlier account.[5]

Reminiscing many years later, Chōgen wrote in *Namuamida-butsu sazenshū*: "Some twenty-three years have passed between the time when, at age sixty-one, I received the imperial order to rebuild Tōdaiji, and now, when I have reached the age of eighty-three. After six years the construction of the Daibutsu was accomplished, and the retired emperor Go Shirakawa paid an imperial visit on the day of the eye-opening [the dedication of the image]" (1934:49). The reference to the imperial order is, to my knowledge, the earliest independent confirmation of the *Zoku yōroku* account. The account is also supported by a passage in the late-Kamakura history *Hyakurenshō*: "On the twenty-sixth day [of the sixth month of 1181], the decision to rebuild Tōdaiji was made, and a petition for assistance was circulated among the Buddhist faithful"(Kuroita 1929:106).

The edict ordering the campaign was clearly the work of Go Shirakawa, though it was formally promulgated by the reigning emperor Antoku, a small boy who of course had nothing to do with it. After the death of Kiyomori, however, Go Shirakawa had reassumed partial control of the state apparatus; thus it was doubtless he who dictated the edict, a contention that may be supported by its laudatory treatment of him. Throughout the document, parallels are drawn between Shōmu's original construction of the temple and the throne's current restoration plans. The edict sometimes quotes directly from Shōmu's proclamation (in the extracts below, direct or near-direct quotations are printed in italics). The document opens with a pious expression of reverence for the imperial line and concern for its preservation (*Tōdaiji zoku yōroku* 1907:199):

> Tender of age as we are, we gratefully laud [past] imperial achievements, rely upon the protection of our ancestors, and earnestly pay heed to the safety of the imperial line. In regard to this, in Yamato province Sofunokami district, there was constructed a great temple with a *jōroku*[6] gilt bronze image that Emperor Shōmu had cast in the Tenpyō era. The roof of the temple soared to the heavens, and the sacred brilliance of the image surpassed that of the full moon; truly there is nothing to compare with it in Japan or China.

When the fires of the Taira laid waste to the temple,

> Zenjō Sen'in [Go Shirakawa] heard of the matter and, deeply moved, had the temple's foundation stones preserved in their original arrangement, trees to reconstruct the building cut in the mountains, a casting mold made by skilled artisans, and copper obtained from the provinces. He desired to rebuild the temple with these materials, and the intent of his imperial vow truly suffices as a grateful response [to Shōmu's establishment of the temple]. *It is We who possess the wealth of the land; it is We who possess all power in the land. With this wealth and power at Our command,* we shall certainly assist others to achieve meditative power and wisdom[7] and shall, moreover, act in accord with the desire expressed long ago by the sainted founder of the temple.

Turning to the matter of financing the rebuilding project, the edict states:

> We ought to appeal to both clergy and lay believers for donations. Since everyone from royalty and ministers of state down to palanquin bearers and low class servants *pays homage daily to the image of Roshana, devotion to the Buddha exists within each heart, and therefore we can construct the image through our own efforts.*[8] Long ago Emperor Shōmu

fervently desired the salvation of all creatures. In his chambers he prayed to the Shintō kami, and publicly he encouraged the world to follow the Buddhist law, graciously issuing imperial orders and accomplishing many good deeds. We must follow such ancient practices and restore this venerable monument! Those who give alms for this purpose, even though it be only a grain of rice, half a penny, a small tool, or a log one foot in length, shall prosper forever and everywhere through the power of their good deeds.

The edict goes on to emphasize further the value of small donations to the project, likening them to small particles that form a great mountain or tiny brooks that make up the ocean. After promising good karma and salvation to donors and peace and prosperity in the realm, the edict, like that of Shōmu, warns its executors: "The officials of the Kinai, the seven circuits, and all the provinces *must not intrude on the people for the sake of this project*" (*Tōdaiji zoku yōroku* 1907:199). In summary, the edict recalls Shōmu's role in the founding of Tōdaiji and quotes directly from his proclamation to emphasize the parallel between him and Go Shirakawa. Furthermore, the edict implies a connection between the welfare of the imperial line and the reconstruction of Tōdaiji; it also points out the responsibility that everyone bears for the project and specifies a broad-based voluntary kanjin campaign to finance it.

The *Zoku yōroku* narrative that contains the edict also establishes a second parallel, between Chōgen and Gyōki. According to the account, when Chōgen first approached Yukitaka to volunteer his services, Yukitaka replied, "In the Tenpyō era, Gyōki Bosatsu was given the imperial order [to rebuild Tōdaiji] and thus proceeded to conduct a kanjin campaign." In his kanjin appeal, moreover, Chōgen declares that when Tōdaiji was founded, "Gyōki Bosatsu brought to fruition the devotion of Buddhist believers" (*Tōdaiji zoku yōroku* 1907:198–200)—much, it is implied, as Chōgen himself intends to do.

Though most Japanese scholars tend to accept the *Zoku yōroku* account, there are reasons to doubt its complete accuracy. Chōgen's appeal carries a bogus date, the eighth month of the first year of Yōwa, but the Yōwa era did not begin until the tenth month. (The imperial order, however, is dated correctly.) Although the incorrect date may have been a later copyist's error, it may also mean that the appeal itself was composed somewhat later, perhaps in order to help form a logical story. In addition, the *Zoku yōroku* account shows none of the floundering that becomes apparent when we read Kanezane's diary. In *Zoku yōroku*, the kanjin campaign began officially in the eighth month, but the imperial order quoted above was dated in the sixth month, indicating that this method of raising revenue had been chosen. But in *Gyokuyō* Go Shirakawa was still wringing his hands in the middle of the seventh month. Kanezane mentioned nothing about Chōgen and the kanjin campaign until the tenth month, when he noted: "The Tōdaiji alms-collecting shōnin (hijiri) went around to all houses in the capital asking for donations—beginning with the retired emperor and not asking whether a household be noble or base. I've heard that the Nyoin [Sutoku's empress and Kanezane's sister, Kōkamon'in] contributed ten catties of bronze and others gave a thousand *kanmon* of cash or six *ryō* of gold" (Kujō 1908, I, 2:532 [1181/10/9]). It may have been his sister's substantial gift that interested Kanezane in the Tōdaiji campaign rather than any importance that he attributed to the kanjin effort itself.

Gyokuyō's record of the stumbling efforts of Go Shirakawa and Kanezane in the middle of 1181 seems somewhat more true to life than the decisive steps described in *Zoku yōroku;* yet the later account should not be dismissed out of hand. Both *Sazenshū* and *Gyokuyō* indicate that an imperial order authorizing a kanjin campaign was in fact promulgated sometime in midyear. The *Zoku yōroku* version probably reflects how the entire effort was meant to be seen, perhaps by Tōdaiji, perhaps by Chōgen, perhaps by Go Shirakawa, but most likely by all three. It was Go Shirakawa, in fact, who had the biggest stake in creating a story of a unified, purposeful effort—a story in which Chōgen played the part of Gyōki and he himself took the role of Emperor Shōmu.

The association of Gyōki with the collection of donations for Tōdaiji, though based on an accepted historical account, seems to have become part of the popular Gyōki legend only after Chōgen's campaign. Heian period sources such as *Hokke genki* and *Konjaku monogatarishū* portray Gyōki as a miracle worker and popular evangelist who helped people in practical ways, for example by building roads and bridges, and whose virtues eventually attracted imperial patronage (Inoue and Ōsone 1974:51–54; Dykstra 1983: 27–29 [book 1, no. 2]; Nagazumi and Ikegami 1966–1968, 1:13–

17 [book 11, no. 2], 27–29 [book 11, no. 7], 3:74–77 [book 17, nos. 36, 37]). But *Shasekishū*, written in the early fourteenth century, identifies him as the "Subscription Saint who took up collections for the construction of Tōdaiji" (Morrell 1985:181; Mujū 1966:256–259 [5B:11]). It is my conjecture that sometime in the process of Chōgen's campaign, the Gyōki legend was embellished with a little-known but probably factual item from the *Shoku nihongi* in an attempt to use popular veneration of Gyōki to validate a widespread kanjin effort.

It is unclear to what extent Chōgen was successful in obtaining donations from ordinary people. His appeal echoes the request for small donations in the imperial edicts of 1181 and 743. Yet there is little information on what ordinary people actually gave; the initial donations noted in *Gyokuyō*, one thousand kanmon of cash or six ryō of gold, are a far cry from a length of cloth. Perhaps the ocean indeed could be formed from the water of tiny brooks, but the contributions of major rivers would fill it up much more efficiently. In addition, if the peasants were as close to starvation as Kanezane claimed, then they would not have had anything to give. It is likely that Tōdaiji received small donations from the general populace but that the most important donors from a practical point of view were people such as Yoritomo, who contributed a thousand bolts of silk, a thousand ryō of gold dust, and ten thousand koku of rice (Hayakawa 1923, 1:112 [1185/3/7]). If the true purpose of the kanjin campaign, however, was to unite people around the throne to rebuild a monument to imperial glory, then it was more important for the campaign to look like a popular effort than to be one.

The Selection of Chōgen

If Go Shirakawa was the catalyst that launched the reconstruction of Tōdaiji, then Chōgen was the force that drove the project to its successful conclusion. His appointment put him in charge not only of the collection of donations, but also of the entire construction process at the temple, a position of great power and influence. The appointment turned out to be a fortunate one for Tōdaiji, since Chōgen was a perspicacious man skilled not only in kanjin methods, but also in shepherding artists, managing revenue, and setting the project's priorities.

The selection of Chōgen requires some explanation. He was an aging monk who had attained no distinguished ecclesiastical rank, had written no commentaries on the scriptures or sophisticated doctrinal treatises, and had no previous connection to Tōdaiji. However, he had already supervised the construction of two temple buildings and had conducted smaller-scale kanjin campaigns, winning the patronage of provincial notables and the devotion of ordinary people.[9] In other words, his technological skill and his ability to attract a wide spectrum of potential donors overcame his relatively low social position and recommended him to court officials such as Yukitaka.

Little is known about Chōgen's life prior to his Tōdaiji appointment. His autobiography, *Namuamidabutsu sazenshū*, primarily concerns his "good deeds" *(sazen)* of constructing temples, images, and baths, but contains a few details about his early life (Chōgen 1934:42–51). Another source is the commentary that he wrote in 1185, on the occasion of the Daibutsu's dedication (*Tōdaiji zoku yōroku* 1907:208–209). Several scholars have used that information, inscriptions, hagiography, and anecdotes to patch together a sketchy picture of his life.[10] He is said to have been born in the capital to a branch of the Ki family with connections to both the Kurōdodokoro and Retired Emperor Toba's guards. Chōgen took Buddhist orders as a boy, perhaps as young as age thirteen, entering the Shingon temple Daigoji on the outskirts of Kyōto. When he was still quite young, he undertook Shugendō practice, traveling to sacred mountains in central Honshū, Shikoku, Kyūshū, and the Tōhoku region, and reciting and copying the Lotus sūtra. He claimed to have traveled to China three times, and it may have been on these travels that he obtained the technological skill that enabled him to design the Daibutsuden.

Like many of his contemporaries, he was devoted to Amida throughout his lifetime. He took credit for making thirty-seven images of Amida, and he eventually adopted the name of Namuamidabutsu, the invocation (nenbutsu) recited by followers of the Pure Land faith. In addition, he advocated chanting the nenbutsu while bathing, and he had baths established at temples and elsewhere, combining practical good work that promoted cleanliness and good health with a ritual that both propagated the nenbutsu and symbolized spiritual cleansing (Gorai 1975:182–185). Biographies of the Pure Land school founder Hōnen claim close connections between him and Chōgen; indeed, both had similar faith in the nenbutsu and a similar concern with popular preaching. Chōgen is most closely associated, however, with the nenbutsu hijiri at Mt. Kōya, where he took up residence sometime before 1176. Scholars have questioned Chōgen's lineage, his exact relationship with Hōnen, and his journeys to China, but the rest of this information is generally accepted and provides a picture of a hijiri like many in late Heian Japan: one who combined mountain asceticism, devotion to Amida and the Lotus sūtra, and construction work that benefited both temples and the general populace.

According to some sources in the Pure Land tradition (e.g., *Kurodani Genkū shōnin den,* quoted in Kobayashi 1971:64), the first choice for the Tōdaiji kanjin position was Hōnen, who declined but recommended Chōgen instead. Though this account may be an invention of Hōnen's hagiographers, it suggests that one important qualification for the head of the kanjin campaign was a closeness to the people of the type that Hōnen and Chōgen had established. Both men, moreover, had developed ties with court functionaries as well as with ordinary folk. They were not merely vagabond hijiri unworthy of official notice, but potential intermediaries between court and populace.

In particular, Chōgen seems to have attracted the patronage of Minamoto Moroyuki, minister of the treasury, a *zuryō* (provincial governor) and client of Retired Emperor Toba (Gomi 1984: 400–403). Moroyuki was the main contributor to a kanjin campaign that Chōgen conducted for the construction of a temple building at Daigoji. In 1176 Chōgen conducted another campaign for a bronze bell at Kōya's Enjuin, dedicated to persons identified as Moroyuki and two of his sons, and to an unidentified nun, probably another family member. One of the sons to whom the bell was dedicated was a monk at Tōdaiji's Tōnan'in (Kobayashi 1971:46), and he may very well have suggested that Chōgen undertake the restoration kanjin project. More generally speaking, the mediation of a powerful functionary such as Moroyuki must have stood Chōgen in good stead in establishing a relationship with the court.

Another useful connection for Chōgen was with the Kurōdo-dokoro, in which Yukitaka held an important position. The connection may have been established through Chōgen's own family or through Moroyuki, who had contacts with the bureau. The Kurōdodokoro had charge of important metal casters' groups, one of which participated in the reconstruction of the Daibutsu and also assisted Chōgen later with such projects as the casting of bath cauldrons at Daigoji and an iron pagoda at Amidaji in Suō province (Amino 1975:365).

Important as Chōgen's connections may have been, it was also his muen status—his lack of *permanent* connections to any single temple, patron, or government office—that made him an appropriate choice to head Go Shirakawa's kanjin campaign. Even after Chōgen assumed responsibility for the Tōdaiji campaign, he remained an outsider whose priorities for reconstruction differed from those of the regular monks (Nagamura 1981:72). Free of entanglements and able to move freely from one social milieu to another, Chōgen—like other hijiri—was in an ideal position to attract donors. In addition, his muen status may have been of value in establishing ties with Go Shirakawa, since muen people had a special relationship to the throne.

According to Amino Yoshihiko, the category muen included not only hijiri but vagabond craftsmen and peddlers as well as the roads they traveled and the ports and markets where they sold their wares (1978b:44). By the late Heian period, as Amino argues elsewhere, the throne had established its jurisdiction over muen people and places (1975:358–367). For example, it granted licenses to certain craftsmen to travel freely without the payment of tolls assessed to most people. In fact, vagabond craftsmen often sought the status of *kugonin* (purveyors to the imperial household), because it would free them from any jurisdiction but that of the throne. Amino points out that Chōgen's right to travel nationwide to collect donations was of the same order as the rights of kugonin (1974:291).

Amino's ideas intersect with those of the anthropologist Yamaguchi Masao, who associates both hijiri and monarch with a type of mythical figure that we may call the Visitor deity (1977:151–179).[11] The Visitor, who appears in various guises, brings both bounty and danger to the isolated village community. As the Japanese terms *hitogami* (human-deity) or *marōdogami* (adventitious deity) indicate, the Visitor was considered to be no ordinary human being, but one who possessed the charisma of a kami. The Visitor—perhaps a deity of a universal religion such as

Buddhism or a famous saint from past history—might bring a community boatloads of grain, chastise the wicked, or mediate between the human and the divine. Sometimes the Visitor was a human being, perhaps a skilled evangelist whose words struck his audience with awe or a ruler who claimed divine descent. His ability to transcend the structures of individual communities gave him power and freedom that insiders—rule- and role-bound—could not muster. Kanjin hijiri often used this ability to their advantage.

Such power and freedom was also possessed in theory by the emperor, with his command over the places and people that lay under no one else's control. In one sense these were "leftover" people and places, outside the structure of agricultural society on which bushi power was based. The affinity between the emperor, who stood above the social structure, and the hijiri, on its margins, should not be pushed too far, but in a sense they both were part of the same extrastructural "system." Hijiri, who traveled freely, both in actual space and from one segment of society to another, were the nodes and channels of a communications network that helped to integrate the whole nation. And that integration, Yamaguchi argues, was precisely the monarch's duty.

Yamaguchi maintains, however, that the monarch "could not manifest his force directly, because it could be antisocial if it were manifested without modification" (1977:157). If this argument is applied to the events of 1181, it appears that Go Shirakawa faced quite a dilemma. Bushi power, which relied more on actual control of provincial land and people than on titles granted by the throne, was threatening the throne's institutional primacy. Thus there was a need for a powerful example of the throne's ability to integrate the nation. The reconstruction of Tōdaiji might fit this need; yet to accomplish it through taxation might be regarded as "antisocial," as Kanezane's objections indicate. The choice of a kanjin campaign, which appeared to be both voluntary and widespread, can be understood in this light. Chōgen, who stood outside the fractured social structure that Go Shirakawa was attempting to transcend and perhaps even to unify, thus appears to be a logical selection to head the campaign.

The Daibutsu Opens Its Eyes

The reconstruction of Tōdaiji was an immense task that took a century to complete. Revenues collected in Chōgen's kanjin campaign played only a small part in financing the project. Additional support was provided by Yoritomo, who assessed "donations" from his vassals with little pretense that they were voluntary gifts, and most importantly by the assignment of revenues from Suō, Bizen, Harima, and Aki provinces. Yet it was the voluntary kanjin campaign that set the tone for the reconstruction effort. For one thing, the initial step in recasting the Daibutsu's head, the construction of the mold, was funded largely through donations collected by Chōgen (Kujō 1908, I, 2:554 [1182/2/20]). Without the campaign, moreover, it would have been difficult for Go Shirakawa to claim that both throne and people had participated in a national effort to reconstruct a monument to imperial glory.

Bronzecasters took more than three years to complete the image, beginning work in the second month of 1183 with the casting of the right hand (Kobayashi 1971:68–75; Amino 1975:364–365). The casting master was a visitor from China, Ch'en Ho-ch'ing, who took on the project at Chōgen's invitation. According to *Gyokuyō*, Ch'en was visiting northern Kyūshū in the summer of 1183 (Kujō 1908, I, 1:567 [1182/7/24]). He was about to return to China when his boat was destroyed, no doubt in one of Kyūshū's frequent typhoons, stranding him in Japan. Ch'en's troubles were Tōdaiji's good fortune, and Chōgen recruited not only him but seven other Chinese casting masters to work with the Japanese bronzecasting team. Ch'en and his seven assistants were joined by fifteen Japanese artisans of the Kusabe group, who had already begun to work with Chōgen on another project. The casting of the Daibutsu's head and neck took thirty days and fourteen passes before it was completed.

In the eighth month of 1185 a dedication ceremony was held for the image of Roshana. The work had been completed with the help of courtiers, bushi, and the common people, who gathered at the ceremony, as "numerous as the sands of the Ganges." Some of them joined the strands of their rosaries together to make a "rope of goodness" to celebrate the occasion (Kujō 1908, II:98 [1185/8/28–30]). Kobayashi Takeshi attributes this unusual example of mass participation in an official temple ceremony to Chōgen's leadership (1971:80–81).

Go Shirakawa himself painted in the eyes of the image. One of Kanezane's companions on the trip home from Nara criticized this conduct as inappropriate: "The retired emperor has become a *busshi* (artist-monk)! What precedent is there for this?" But another replied, "The precedent is from the Tenpyō era, when Emperor Shōmu took the brush himself and deigned to paint in the eyes [of the original Daibutsu]" (Kujō 1908, II:98 [1185/8/28–30]). A side note adds that Shōmu was retired at the time. It seems likely that this story, which is not the standard account, was promoted by Go Shirakawa in an attempt to identify himself with Shōmu and the twelfth-century throne with the throne in its glory days of the eighth.

Religious legitimation of the throne's authority must have seemed as important to Go Shirakawa in 1185 as it did in 1181. Even though he had eventually thrown his support to Yoritomo, Go Shirakawa was in a precarious position after the Minamoto victory over the Taira at Dannoura. Yoritomo's refusal to permit his followers to accept court appointments without his permission clearly established his independent authority over the bushi in the Kantō (eastern Japan). Thus Go Shirakawa had failed to make Yoritomo his client, and a new bushi leader posed a challenge to court and throne. Later that year, the retired emperor turned for support to Yoritomo's brother Yoshitsune, but neither that move nor the reconstruction of Tōdaiji succeeded in restoring the throne to the position it had held in Shōmu's day. Perhaps the respectful treatment of emperor and court by the early rulers of Kamakura rested in part, however, on Kamakura's knowledge that no bushi leader of the age could claim a relationship to the entire nation comparable to that of the throne.

Chōgen and Yoritomo

Even in the first few years of the construction project, however, Go Shirakawa had to share sponsorship with warrior leaders such as Yoritomo, who had even more time and energy to devote to temple building after his victory over the Taira in 1185. Moreover, the reconstruction of Tōdaiji fit Yoritomo's political agenda, just as it had fit that of Go Shirakawa. Yoritomo's assistance can be seen as an attempt to gain political capital by helping to restore what the Taira had destroyed. The cooperation of court and warrior leaders served the purposes of both: the court benefited when warriors paid public homage to the system of aristocratic rulership in which Tōdaiji played a part, and warriors benefited because they could claim to be the defenders of legitimate authority. As for

Chōgen, he must have been grateful for Yoritomo's help. Chief of the warriors that had won the Genpei war and thus the nation's leading military power, Yoritomo was an invaluable aid in any case, but certainly crucial to the project's success after the deaths of Yukitaka in 1187 and Go Shirakawa in 1192.

In 1184, with the Daibutsu well on its way to completion, Chōgen turned to his next project, a building (the Daibutsuden) to house the great image. If the Daibutsu had been a huge project, this building was an immense one, requiring the collection of materials such as timber, stone, and tile; the mobilization of persons skilled in architecture, engineering and shipping; and the management of land and other resources. Yoritomo was Chōgen's main lay support in constructing the edifice (Horiike 1976:9).

Chōgen once again proved himself equal to a difficult task. Through ties with political authorities, artists, and fellow monks, the Tōdaiji kanjin hijiri constructed both a personal network of supporters and a physical network of branch temples and shōen to sustain his endeavors. In addition to having the Daibutsuden and other temple buildings reconstructed, Chōgen helped to create an official position at Tōdaiji that was responsible for construction projects and other economic matters for many years to come.

The construction of the Daibutsuden took eleven years to accomplish, from 1184 when Chōgen first began to search for timber for the project to 1195 when the grand dedication ceremony was held.[12] Chōgen's first task was to find suitable timber, and this was not easy. First he turned to the Yoshino mountains and then to the mountain behind Ise shrine, appealing to the shrine's kami Amaterasu by dedicating a sūtra to her. Chōgen's real audience was no doubt the court, which venerated Amaterasu as the ancestor of the imperial family. For unspecified reasons, Chōgen's initial efforts were unsuccessful. Suitable materials were finally obtained from Suō province in southwest Honshū, through the help of both Go Shirakawa and Yoritomo.

In 1186 Suō was granted to Tōdaiji as a proprietary province: all revenues from Suō's public lands were directed toward Tōdaiji's reconstruction. Two factors made Suō a suitable choice: first, it had abundant forests, and second, it was under the direct control of Go Shirakawa, the de facto "chairman" of the rebuilding project. Chōgen was put in charge of the province, and in 1186 he led a team of artisans, including the Daibutsu casting master

Ch'en Ho-ch'ing, to survey the forests. According to an inscription on an iron stupa at Suō Amidaji, a temple Chōgen built there, "logging operations for the reconstruction of Tōdaiji began on Bunji 2 (1186)/4/18" (Kobayashi 1971:90).

The project soon ran into trouble, partly because it was difficult and expensive to transport logs from Suō all the way to Nara. Numerous dams—perhaps as many as one hundred—were built along the Saba river to facilitate the effort to float logs downstream. Expenses overran revenue, and it became necessary to donate Bizen and Harima province income to Tōdaiji in 1193, the year before the Daibutsuden was completed. Other difficulties came from local Suō warriors, and Yoritomo had to warn them on several occasions not to interfere with the shipping of timber. In the third month of 1187, Chōgen complained that jitō appointed by Kamakura had seized rice needed to feed laborers on the project and had physically obstructed the logging operation (Takeuchi 1971–1991, 1:129–130 [doc. 210]). In a communiqué apparently addressed to Go Shirakawa, Yoritomo declared his support for the reconstruction project and suggested that, rather than relying on a single province (Suō), Tōdaiji should tap all provinces and secure funding from the retired emperor, the court, and all landholders through a levy on every shōen (Takeuchi 1971–1991, 1:133–134 [doc. 219]). In other words, Yoritomo was recommending a nationwide tax. On a smaller scale, in 1190 Yoritomo required his goke'nin (vassals) in the Kantō to donate rope (or the funds to buy it) to the Tōdaiji effort, an "indirect kanjin" method employing a political structure under Kamakura's control (Nagamura 1981:70).

Why did Yoritomo support the reconstruction of Tōdaiji? In his missive to Go Shirakawa, he pointed out that the Taira, enemies of the court, had destroyed Tōdaiji and that it was necessary to reconstruct the temple quickly. Thus assistance had to be provided without fail. Yoritomo charged Go Shirakawa with responsibility for the restoration of the temple, "built by Shōmu's command." If these were words that Go Shirakawa wanted to hear, they were no doubt also words that Yoritomo wanted to say: he had linked the destruction of the Taira, the rebuilding of Tōdaiji, and the restoration of the glory of the throne to that of Shōmu's time and had promoted himself as the true agent of all three tasks.

Yoritomo's political agenda differed from that of Go Shirakawa. The retired emperor wanted to integrate the nation with the throne at its center; Yoritomo was more concerned with establishing control over the other bushi. Though Yoritomo's aim was the more limited one, it did require efforts to legitimize his authority such as restoring and supporting religious institutions. Tōdaiji was not Yoritomo's sole religious project. As Jeffrey P. Mass points out, when Yoritomo was consolidating his power in eastern Japan in 1180, he took upon himself the role of protector of temples and shrines, seizing public land and granting it to Mishima shrine in Izu; this was "in marked contrast to the Taira, who were consistently seeking to outdo their central religious rivals in the competition for land profits" (1974a:137). In 1187, moreover, Yoritomo ordered notables and officials of Shinano province to cooperate with kanjin efforts at Zenkōji (Takeuchi 1971–1991, 1:146–147 [docs. 248, 249]). The command was sent to all *sata'nin* (a term that probably refers, in this case, to Yoritomo's warrior vassals) on shōen and public land; they were threatened with confiscation of their holdings if they failed to cooperate. Another of Yoritomo's orders, this time in 1191, authorized a kanjin campaign by Tōji (Takeuchi 1971–1991, 2:454 [doc. 567]). Like Tōdaiji, Zenkōji and Tōji were venerable and powerful temples, and Yoritomo must have thought that supporting them would lend legitimacy to his power over others in the warrior class as well as to his claim to be the protector of aristocratic interests.

Perhaps because Yoritomo's aims were different from Go Shirakawa's, he does not seem to have been so anxious to rebuild Tōdaiji through a voluntary kanjin campaign. In the edict that Go Shirakawa authored in 1181, he was careful to suggest that Tōdaiji be restored by such a campaign—an attempt, as I have argued, to *appear* to have won the willing cooperation of his subjects. Yoritomo, however, headed a military structure that was under no constraint to avoid the appearance of force. In fact, it probably heightened his authority when other military men meekly did what they were told. Thus it was not crucial for him to sponsor a voluntary kanjin campaign, and coercion could be applied to obtain the cooperation of military subordinates in temple-building projects. Unlike Go Shirakawa, Yoritomo did not try to disguise his use of force. Thus the image of a nationwide voluntary kanjin campaign that was so important for Go Shirakawa's purposes was not necessary for those of Yoritomo.

It is important to remember that Tōdaiji's reconstruction was not solely the doing of Chōgen, Go Shirakawa, and Yoritomo. Rather, it was accomplished through the cooperation of all important elements in Japanese society: the court, the military, the Buddhist clergy both regular and marginal, and, above all, the people themselves. The kanjin campaign had become a vehicle to forge a symbiosis between temple and community, in this case the entire nation; if both throne and bakufu profited from that symbiosis, so did the cause to which Chōgen was devoted, the dissemination of Buddhist teachings. Even though the material contribution of the kanjin campaign to Tōdaiji's reconstruction may have been a small one, without it the undertaking would have been just another elite project. Popular participation helped to restore not only Tōdaiji's images and buildings, but its claim to be the religious center of the entire nation.

Chōgen and Construction of the Bessho

Perhaps in accord with his new patron's approach, Chōgen spent less time collecting donations than he had before and more planning the construction project and managing the materials and revenue to support it. Much of his effort was devoted to establishing seven provincial temples, or bessho, that helped to support the Tōdaiji project.[13] As the name *bessho* indicates, the temples were "separate places" that served the main temple. The seven bessho included five in Inland Sea provinces, from Suō in the west to Settsu in the east; one in Iga, where Tōdaiji had extensive holdings; and one on the precincts of Tōdaiji itself (see Table 2 for a list of the bessho).

Chōgen's seven bessho served practical needs of the kanjin campaign and the Tōdaiji reconstruction project. The earliest one, Jōdodō, was probably established on the precincts of Tōdaiji sometime between 1185 and 1187, in the early years of the effort to reconstruct the Daibutsuden.[14] Jōdodō, which included a bath and a dining hall as well as a central building with ten images of Amida, was probably Chōgen's base of operations and lodging for the hijiri who helped Chōgen in his work. The second bessho to be established, Amidaji in Suō, was probably built in 1186 or 1187, shortly after Tōdaiji had been authorized to exploit the province's revenues. From Amidaji, Chōgen or his delegates could oversee

Table 2 The Bessho and Their Functions in Tōdaiji Reconstruction

Name	Location	Founded*	Contents	Rites	Functions	Buildings**
Jōdodō	Nara: Tōdaiji	1185–1187	Ten Amidas, relics	nenbutsu	kanjin base	bath, dining hall
Amidaji	Suō	1186–1187	Amida	nenbutsu, bathing nenbutsu	oversee logging operations	bath, relic hall
Jōdoji	Harima: Ōbe shō	1192–1193	Amida triad	raigō	oversee shōen	bath
Watanabe	Settsu: Tenmabashi	1186–1197	Amida triad	raigō	lumber storage	Raigōdō, Shabadō, bath
Jōdodō	Bitchū	> 1193?	Amida		oversee tile making?	
Jōgyōdō	Bizen	> 1193?	Amida		oversee tile making?	
Shindaibutsuji	Iga	1197–1202	Amida triad, stone Jizō		oversee shōen	bath

*Dates are approximate; > means after.

**Each bessho had a Jōdodō, dedicated to Amida, as its central worship hall.

timbering operations, including the difficult task of floating logs down the nearby Saba river. In addition, kanjin activities required a presence in Suō, where there was trouble with provincial bushi. From the other bessho, Chōgen and his associates were able to supervise crucial facets of the reconstruction project. The Settsu bessho at Watanabe, between Tenmabashi and Tenjinbashi in present Ōsaka, was the location of a storage shed for logs shipped up the Inland Sea from Suō. The functions of Jōdodō in Bitchū and Jōgyōdō in Bizen are not so certain. They were probably founded sometime after Bizen became Tōdaiji's proprietary province in 1193. Archaeological findings indicate that the temples were located near a kiln that made tiles for the roofs of Tōdaiji buildings: a roof tile discovered in the vicinity bears the inscription "Kibitsu Miya Jōgyōdō" and resembles tiles used for the Daibutsuden. Monks at the two bessho may have supervised the kiln or warehouses where tiles were stored before they were shipped to Tōdaiji. The temples may have also served as bases for Chōgen's construction activities in the region, which included kanjin efforts throughout Bizen to improve the mountain road on the Bizen-Harima border, the most dangerous section of the Sanyō highway. The road was no doubt used to transport materials from Bizen's interior to ports on the Inland Sea and thence to Tōdaiji.

The Harima (Jōdoji) and Iga (Shindaibutsuji) bessho were situated on Tōdaiji shōen, and their main function may have been to supervise these holdings. The Harima bessho was established in 1192, as part of Chōgen's attempt to restore Ōbe shō, a neglected Tōdaiji holding. The shōen is located near the Kako river, and one function of the temple may have been as a storehouse for materials that were later floated downriver to larger boats on the Inland Sea. It was probably to improve shipping conditions for these materials that Chōgen conducted a kanjin campaign to repair the anchorage at Uozumi in Harima province. Shindaibutsuji, located far from any convenient transportation routes, appears to have played no role in the shipping of materials to Tōdaiji, but as Kobayashi Takeshi suggests, it may have been intended to oversee Tōdaiji's four shōen in the area, which had been plagued with management problems that hindered their usefulness to the temple (1971:234).

In summary, Chōgen's bessho served various functions connected with Tōdaiji's reconstruction: they housed kanjin hijiri; they were offices from which to oversee Tōdaiji shōen, logging operations, or the making of roof tiles; and they stored materials on their way to Tōdaiji. These temples, along with a bessho that Chōgen had established at Mt. Kōya before his Tōdaiji appointment, can help to define the geographical area in which he worked and to indicate the scope of his activities.

Chōgen took a strong personal interest in the bessho, sometimes even participating physically in their construction. According to one account of the origin of the Suō bessho, "Chōgen himself cleared away the brambles and, taking hoe in hand, finished the work in three days and three nights" (*Chōgen shōnin chigan no ki*, quoted in Nakao 1977:185). Chōgen discussed the building of the Harima bessho in a communiqué dated 1192: he collected materials from some abandoned temples nearby and constructed a building, adorning it with several images and naming it Namuamida-butsuji (Kobayashi 1971:250-251). This building became the nucleus of Jōdoji, a temple complex completed several years later. Its Jōdodō—the only extant structure there that dates from Chōgen's time—was built in the same architectural style as the Daibutsuden and contained gilded images of Amida and two attendants. In a slightly different version of the story written five years later in his testament, Chōgen relates that he built a second chapel, the Yakushidō, to the same specifications as the Jōdodō and installed within it some eight hundred old images of buddhas and bodhisattvas, all found in the abandoned temples (Takeuchi 1971-1991, 2:229-233 [doc. 920]).

As for Shindaibutsuji, Chōgen wrote in his *Namuamidabutsu Sazenshū* that he began construction by first choosing an auspicious spot, then removing boulders to level the area (1934:46). The temple's altars and pedestals were made of stone, possibly these very boulders. The central building, the Amidadō, contained an Amida triad, and its back doors opened onto a cliff where an image of Jizō had been carved. The relatively detailed description in *Sazenshū* suggests that Chōgen had special affection for this temple.

The bessho were significant in the religious lives of Chōgen and his followers, and they played an important role in the spread of his Pure Land ideas. Amida was the honzon at every bessho and at several of them, the focus of public ceremonies that may have provided occasions for collecting kanjin donations. In constructing the bessho, Chōgen established a network of temples that connected the Pure Land faith firmly with Tōdaiji. No better method could have been used to focus popular religious attention on the great temple in Nara.

The ceremonies conducted at the bessho were of two main types: *raigō* ceremonies, depicting Amida's welcome to the dying, and the chanting of the nenbutsu by hijiri, often while they were bathing. According to *Sazenshū*, the raigō ceremony was first performed at the Settsu bessho in 1197, with twenty-five men costumed as attendant bodhisattvas and with the temple's main images, an Amida triad, "playing" the starring roles of Amida and his two main attendants, the bodhisattvas Kannon and Seishi (Chōgen 1934:45; Tanaka 1976:38–39). The living actors, beating drums—one of which is extant—proceeded from the raigō hall (Raigōdō), which represented Amida's paradise, to the *shaba* hall (Shabadō), which represented the ordinary world where the faithful lay dying. At the Harima bessho, raigō ceremonies initiated in 1200 were focused on an image of Amida attributed to the famous Nara sculptor Kaikei, who had close ties to Chōgen (Tanaka 1976:37). In this ceremony the image was clad in robes and carried across a pond that separated the Jōdodō from the Yakushidō, representing the ordinary world.

Sazenshū notes that baths were constructed at five of the seven Tōdaiji bessho (Chōgen 1934:45–46). They were sites of the bathing nenbutsu ritual, in which hijiri chanted the name of Amida and cleansed themselves spiritually as well as physically. The hijiri who gathered at Suō Amidaji included twelve hijiri in a nenbutsu group and six others in a bathing group, all with names ending with *amidabutsu*, the mark of Chōgen's disciples (Kobayashi 1971:201). Some of the baths were for the hijiri only, but the Watanabe bessho also had a bath for public use, and perhaps other bessho did too (Gorai 1975:182; Horiike 1976:16). Thus people might cleanse themselves and at the same time listen to hijiri chanting the nenbutsu. It seems unlikely that Chōgen and his followers passed up such opportunities to collect donations for the reconstruction of the Daibutsuden. Chōgen probably encouraged bathing by promoting its spiritual benefits, but he was a practical man and must also have recognized the contribution of his baths to public hygiene.

Like Gyōki before him and a multitude of kanjin hijiri who followed, Chōgen combined construction work with the teaching of Buddhism. Chōgen may have wanted to identify himself with Gyōki by following in the footsteps of the first Tōdaiji kanjin hijiri, and he must have known that public gratitude for construction projects was often expressed as financial support for temples. In addition, he may have been trying to help his powerful patrons establish control over strategically important regions by developing transportation facilities there.

When Chōgen described some of his projects in *Sazenshū*, he made a point of linking himself with Gyōki. The anchorage that Chōgen repaired at Uozumi, for instance, was "constructed by Gyōki in order to help people." Describing another of his projects, Chōgen wrote: "The Saruyama irrigation pond in Kawachi province is a historic monument to Gyōki Bosatsu; however, its dikes had crumbled and I repaired it in order to protect the surrounding fields and mountain land" (Chōgen 1934:49–50). In both instances, Chōgen not only claimed that he was following in Gyōki's footsteps but pointed out the public benefit of his and Gyōki's deeds. It was the potent combination of religion and public service that endeared kanjin hijiri to local communities and their leaders and served as a vehicle for the wide dissemination of Buddhist ideas. Lay believers may very well have donated to Tōdaiji because they were grateful for the repair of a useful anchorage or the construction of a highway.

It should be noted, moreover, that much of Chōgen's construction activity—both temples and secular projects—took place in the vital Inland Sea region. It was there, Amino Yoshihiko argues, that thirteenth-century monks associated with the bakufu helped their patrons establish control over shipping routes and highways (1974:297–302). Amino's argument should perhaps be extended backward in time. If so, then Yoritomo's patronage of Chōgen takes on another dimension.

Yoritomo had considerable reason to be concerned with the Inland Sea region. It had been the base of the Taira—they had even moved the capital briefly from Kyōto to Fukuhara near present Kōbe—and thus was a possible locus of dissatisfaction with Kamakura's control of the warrior class. When the bakufu imposed jitō on the shōen, they were initially placed on confiscated Taira estates in western Japan, including the Inland Sea region. Coastal shipping and land transportation along the coast, moreover, were of vital importance to central shōen proprietors in Kyōto and Nara, who depended on western estates for much of their income. Thus it seems likely that when Go Shirakawa and Yoritomo encouraged Chōgen's activities in the Inland Sea region, they had more in mind than simply assisting the reconstruction of Tōdaiji. The temple's receipt of revenues from the public lands in Suō, Bizen, Harima, and Aki provinces should probably be seen in this light, as should the considerable executive powers given to Chōgen in Suō, where he was the de facto provincial governor. Under his direction, the kanjin office heard lawsuits and issued rights to income from public land (Nagamura 1980:55–56). Peter Arnesen suggests that Chōgen was not officially appointed governor because there was no precedent for a monk occupying such a post but that the nominal governor, a civilian aristocrat, was forbidden to interfere with Tōdaiji's administration of the province (1982:105).

If Chōgen's success in rebuilding Tōdaiji came as much from his skills in managing resources and negotiating political agreements as from his ability to attract donors, the kanjin method remained central to his enterprise and was used in a variety of ways. In 1205 he issued a public appeal to people to "donate" their young sons to recite the Lotus sūtra at Tōdaiji and presumably to enter monastic life (Takeuchi 1971–1991, 3:263–264 [doc. 1592]). He also conducted kanjin campaigns for public works projects, such as the improvement of roads, irrigation ponds, and anchorages. In addition, men who appear to have been Chōgen's disciples also participated in kanjin projects of their own. A communiqué dated 1200, describing a kanjin campaign for the construction of an Amida chapel at Iga Jōrakuji, was signed by Sen'amidabutsu (Takeuchi 1971–1991, 2:397 [doc. 1149]), and Son'amidabutsu issued a kanjin appeal to rebuild Chōkyūji in 1208 (Takeuchi 1971–1991, 3:370 [doc. 1771]). Kanjin campaigns may not have produced the revenue of, say, all the public lands in the province of Suō, but they were still a significant method of attracting wide participation in crucial temple projects.

The Tōdaiji Daikanjinshiki

Chōgen's central position in Tōdaiji reconstruction was formalized in his appointment as the first Tōdaiji daikanjinshiki, an office charged with the temple's reconstruction. Though others before him had held similar positions at other temples, it was Chō-gen who did the most to broaden the definition of the term to embrace vast responsibilities for management and construction as well as for alms collecting.

The term *daikanjin* was in use in the Heian period, but it usually referred simply to the head of a group—or even just a pair—of kanjin hijiri. For example, donations for the engraving of sūtra passages on copper plates buried in 1142 in Buzen province were collected by two hijiri, one listed as daikanjin (chief solicitor) and the other as *shōkanjin* (assistant solicitor) (Nara Kokuritsu Haku-butsukan 1973: no. 33). These were not official titles, and presumably anyone could call himself daikanjin.

When the court granted the title of daikanjin, however, it was attached to a *shiki*. The term *shiki* originally meant an office but later came to signify the right to income due an officeholder, with or without duties to perform (Mass 1976:208). Rights to shōen income, for instance, were called shiki, and these rights eventually became heritable and alienable. Even in such cases, the term was still an official one, since it was guaranteed by the court, or later, by Kamakura. The first instance of a daikanjinshiki that I have encountered was in the appointment of Enshō to that post at Nen-butsu Sanmaiin at Shitennōji in 1154. Enshō received the title from Retired Emperor Toba along with rights to all offices within the temple in question and jurisdiction over the temple's shōen (Takeuchi 1963–1976, 11:309 [supp. doc. 328]). Although the daikanjinshiki was in existence before the Kamakura period, it does not appear to have been granted very often.

Chōgen and his successors were appointed to the Tōdaiji daikanjinshiki by the court. It is not clear when the first appointment was made. The list of Tōdaiji daikanjinshiki holders compiled by Nagamura Makoto gives Chōgen's appointment date as 1181 (1981:65), and conventional wisdom would indeed support this date, since it was then that he began his work on behalf of the temple. According to Nakanodō Isshin, however, neither Chō-gen nor his contemporaries referred to him as daikanjin before the summer of 1197, and thus he probably did not receive the appointment much before that date (1975:45–48). Nakanodō's argument has considerable merit, since it seems unlikely that Chō-gen, never modest about his accomplishments, would be reluctant to use his official title.

Throughout his tenure at Tōdaiji, Chōgen exercised authority independently from the temple's internal governing body, the monks' assembly (Nagamura 1981:72). Neither Chōgen nor his immediate successors as daikanjinshiki were Tōdaiji monks, and the authority of the daikanjinshiki, like that of the bettō in earlier days, came directly from the court. (The support of the bakufu was crucial in rendering that authority effective.) The division of authority gave rise to a rift between Chōgen and the monks, demonstrated first of all by Chōgen's choice of heirs to the management of the bessho and the shōen holdings that had been placed in his charge.

According to his testament of 1197, Chōgen had originally wanted to bequeath his holdings to Nyoamidabutsu Shōken, a Shingon monk from Daigoji and chief monk of Tōnan'in, a Tōdaiji subtemple of the Shingon line (Takeuchi 1971–1991, 2:229–233 [doc. 920]). Shōken had helped Chōgen with the Tōdaiji project (Horiike 1976:13), and the reconstruction of Tōnan'in, destroyed in 1180 along with the main temple, was one of Chōgen's priorities. Thus the two men were undoubtedly quite close. When Shōken died, however, his successor at Tōnan'in, Gan'amidabutsu Jōhan, became Chōgen's heir. Like both Chōgen and Shōken, Jōhan was a Shingon monk originally from Daigoji.

Chōgen's will placed the shōen in Iga, Harima, Suō, and Bizen under Jōhan's control. He also bequeathed to Jōhan management of the bessho at Tōdaiji and Watanabe, and in Harima province; the lumber storage facilities at Watanabe; and the bessho at Mt. Kōya, which had no apparent connection to the Tōdaiji reconstruction project. The other bessho are not specifically mentioned, but if they were located on the designated shōen, then they would have been included.

Nakao Takashi suggests that Chōgen intended to guarantee that his kanjin hijiri group maintain control over these important properties (1977:181). Chōgen wrote in the testament: "The above-mentioned temple shōen and structures were established and managed by Namuamidabutsu for the sole purpose of spreading the Buddhist law and benefiting all creatures. Now, however, I am approaching eighty years of age. . . . I decided to bequeath these holdings to Shōken of Tōnan'in so that the Buddhist projects that I initiated will be preserved in the future and managed with-

out neglect." Chōgen goes on to tell of Shōken's death and his subsequent choice of Jōhan, and he stipulates that in the future the
holdings be passed on in Jōhan's monastic line: "By no means
should these properties be divided among other lineages or put
under the control of Tōdaiji's bettō or its monks' cabinet, for this
would eventually become the cause for decline." Later on in the
testament Chōgen relates the history of the Harima bessho, telling
how he reclaimed the fields surrounding the temple and earmarked their produce for its support. "[This produce] should not
be used to pay levies to the main temple [Tōdaiji]; it would be better to let the fields lie fallow than to have their profits constantly
diverted into private hands" (Takeuchi 1971–1991, 2:229–233
[doc. 920]).

The testament makes clear that Chōgen deeply distrusted the
Tōdaiji officials and thought that they would misuse the bessho
and shōen for their personal profit. In fact, one of the evils that the
Nara revival aimed to combat was the appropriation of monastic
holdings, which were often passed down to designated heirs as if
they were private property. Ironically, Chōgen also chose a personal associate as his heir. However, his testament did not leave
the welfare of his favorite religious institutions to chance, and the
income from the shōen was earmarked bushel by bushel for specific services at the bessho and at the Daibutsuden, the Kaidan'in,
and the Hachiman shrine at Tōdaiji.

The rift between Chōgen and the regular Tōdaiji monks is
demonstrated by the open quarrel that took place over construction priorities in 1201. Once the corridor of the Daibutsuden was
finished, the monks wanted next to construct a residence and a
lecture hall, but Chōgen preferred to build a pagoda first. Though
the monks petitioned the court, Chōgen's wishes prevailed.
According to Nagamura Makoto, the quarrel points out the fundamental differences between the kanjin hijiri Chōgen, with his
attachment to relics (the contents of a pagoda), and the monks,
with their interest in restoring their own operational base within
the temple (1981:72).

The question of Chōgen's official title—whether it was
granted in 1181, 1197, or sometime in between—may well be
linked to these differences with the monks. If the granting of the
title was indeed delayed, it may have been because the Tōdaiji
monks resisted the regularization of Chōgen's status. It seems

likely that the office, which gave Chōgen security but probably did not destroy his independence, was more to his advantage than to that of the Tōdaiji monks. The monks, in fact, may have wanted to maintain the ad hoc basis of Chōgen's appointment as long as possible, in order to prevent yet another outside appointee from meddling in their affairs. If so, they must have viewed the quarrel of 1201 and Chōgen's eventual victory with considerable dissatisfaction. With varying degrees of success, the monks' assembly tried to influence subsequent appointments to the daikanjinshiki. Like many other temples, Tōdaiji in the late Kamakura period sought to fill the daikanjin position with monks who followed Zen or Ritsu teachings; these monks were considered particularly honest and free from the entanglements that might prevent them from devoting themselves wholeheartedly to Tōdaiji's interests (Nagamura 1981:81). Both the Tōdaiji monks and Chōgen were concerned about the diversion of temple funds into private hands, but each had different perceptions of the problem and its solution.

Even if the daikanjinshiki was not granted to Chōgen until 1197, his functions were extensive prior to that date. Besides broadened responsibilities related directly to Tōdaiji's rebuilding —the mobilization of labor and the setting of construction priorities in addition to the securing of donations—Chōgen's office also handled unprecedented official duties, especially in Suō. He was the first kanjin hijiri to exercise public authority on any substantial scale. Even though daikanjinshiki appointments were subsequently made for other temples such as Shitennōji and the complex at Kōya (Nagamura 1981:62), Chōgen's responsibilities remained atypical, since no temple other than Tōdaiji could claim the nationwide allegiance due a monument of the imperial throne. The Tōdaiji daikanjinshiki remains the pinnacle of cooperation between the state and a kanjin solicitor who retained elements of muen status throughout his life.

Taking Amida's Name

Chōgen's success in rebuilding Tōdaiji was due in part to his ability to mobilize the talents of metal casters, sculptors, and fellow hijiri. The casting of the Daibutsu, the construction of baths, the carving of wooden and stone images at Tōdaiji and the bessho, the collection of materials for Tōdaiji and other projects, and the supervision of estates that supplied the temple were all accomplished with the assistance of Chōgen's friends and disciples. Crucial to the project's success was the casting master Ch'en Hoch'ing. Like Chōgen, Ch'en was a man of many talents: he also helped to oversee timbering operations in Suō, and he held nominal control over several temple shōen, although their actual management fell to Chōgen. Other Chinese artists were also involved in the Tōdaiji project, including the sculptor of the pair of stone lions at the Nandaimon (Great South Gate), carved in 1196 (Kobayashi 1971:148). This man is sometimes identified as I Yukisue (this is the Japanese pronunciation of his name), known as the founder of a school of stone Buddhist sculptors that was active in the Nara region.

Some of Chōgen's relationships were no doubt contractual and temporary, but others were close ones based on common religious practices, in particular the recital of the nenbutsu. A case in point is the famous sculptor Kaikei (see Mōri 1976:67–74), who carved the honzon of Harima Jōdoji and Shindaibutsuji, the guardian figures at Tōdaiji's Nandaimon, and the kami Hachiman at Tōdaiji.[15] Kaikei followed Chōgen's practice of incorporating Amida's name into his own: while Chōgen was Namuamidabutsu, Kaikei was An'amidabutsu. Chōgen's other associates included such men as Kan'amidabutsu, Tokuamidabutsu, Hōamidabutsu, and Jūamidabutsu. This practice followed standard naming customs in which a portion of a father's or a lord's name was bestowed upon a son or a follower, but in these cases the practice also had religious implications.

The Tendai abbot Jien viewed the adoption of the *amida* suffix as an act of arrogance and incorrectly blamed the practice on the influence of Hōnen:

There were such incidents as Shunjō [Chōgen] of Tōdai Temple claiming that he was an incarnation of Amitābha [Amida] and giving himself the name of "Glorious Amitābha Buddha." Many others received names that were made up of "Amitābha Buddha" preceded by a Chinese character. . . . In time, the activity of persons who called themselves the disciples of Hōnen left no doubt but that Buddhist Law had really reached its "deterioriating phase." (Brown and Ishida 1979:172; Jien 1969:521)

There is no indication that Chōgen actually considered himself Amida's reincarnation, and the passage probably reflects the prejudice of a Tendai cleric against the burgeoning Pure Land movement that was not under Tendai control. Rather, the *amida* suffix should be seen as an emblem of membership in a collectivity that had a common religious purpose.

When Chōgen formed this collectivity, he placed himself at the center and at first included only his intimates. Later he broadened the collectivity to embrace donors to his projects. In 1187 he signed an inscription on an armrest with the name Namuamidabutsu; this signature is the earliest evidence of his adoption of the *amida* suffix (Mizukami 1969:340). Subsequently Kaikei and many of Chōgen's other associates added the suffix to their own religious names. These men played important parts in all aspects of Tōdaiji operations (Nakao 1977; Wata 1976:113–117). Chōgen's nephew Kan'amidabutsu, who had participated in the kanjin campaign, took charge of the Harima bessho and Ōbe estate. Other names with the *amida* suffix appear in official capacities at the other bessho and at the Tōdaiji shōen developed and managed by Chōgen. The designated heirs to Chōgen's management rights over shōen and bessho both used the *amida* suffix.

Registers of donors found within several images carved by Kaikei between 1201 and 1203 also include many with the *amida* suffix (Mōri 1976:68–70). The images were made with the help of numerous donors: fifty people contributed for the Amida at the Harima bessho, one hundred fifty for the Tōdaiji Hachiman, and more than sixty for the Shindaibutsuji Amida. According to *Sazenshū*, in 1202 Chōgen began to bestow the suffix "on noble and base, high and low throughout the nation of Japan" (Chōgen 1934:50). The name registers within Kaikei's images, however, indicate that Chōgen began this practice somewhat earlier and that it was a kanjin device. Mizukami Ichikyū suggests that bestowing the suffix on donors gave Chōgen a chance to spread the nenbutsu faith while seeking donations to Tōdaiji (1969:340–343). Besides conferring the suffix, he seems to have distributed amulets to donors, no doubt as visible tokens of both their gifts to the Tōdaiji cause and their guarantee of salvation in the next world.

The use of the *amida* suffix helped to define a group of associates and supporters that had formed a community based on religious aims. Kanjin hijiri, estate managers, artists, and donors signified their membership in the community by adopting a common element for their names. In addition, as Mizukami suggests, this gave Chōgen and others the opportunity to chant the nenbutsu, a key factor in popular Amidist practice. Donating to Tōdaiji and the invocation of Amida merged in a single religious practice.

Mizukami argues that many of the lay donors to Tōdaiji and other projects who assumed the *amida* suffix were local landholders and points out that the suffix became quite common in the Kinai region in areas surrounding Hōryūji as well as Tōdaiji (1969:357–358). The adoption of the suffix was related to kanjin activities at Hōryūji and elsewhere. For example, the kanjin *bikuni* (nun) Jōamidabutsu collected donations for Hōryūji in 1236, and contributors to a variety of kanjin efforts signed donation registers with the *amidabutsu* name. That women as well as men adopted the suffix indicates that even gender distinctions might blur in pursuit of religious community.

The practice among local landholders, according to Mizukami, reflects the fact that many temple monks came from a landholding milieu; more than that, I would argue, it reflects the common interests that temples and landholders had in constructing a community and the physical structures that made that community a reality. The cooperation between temples and local landholders, a phenomenon that I will discuss in the following chapter, relied not only on kinship ties but also on the mutual advantage that each found in pursuing a common aim.

Chōgen and Jōkei

Among the many "good deeds" that Chōgen recorded in *Sazenshū* were several valuable gifts to Kasagidera: a copy of the Dai Hannya sūtra that he had brought back from China; a white sandalwood image of Shakyamuni, "the honzon of Emperor Shōmu"; and a bronze bell that remains at Kasagidera today (Chōgen 1934: 50). The bell is inscribed with Chōgen's vow: "This newly cast temple bell shall make the Buddhist law resound in distant places. I pray that all beings develop the will for enlightenment," and signed with the name Namuamidabutsu (Kobayashi 1971:315).

Chōgen's gifts were in response to the Kasagidera kanjin effort, and he and Jōkei maintained a close relationship despite their obvious differences in social class, doctrinal sophistication, and religious style. In the scholarly monk who assumed the functions of a kanjin hijiri and the kanjin hijiri who managed the affairs of Japan's greatest temple, we see the two faces of the Nara revival. The two men are apt representatives of a complex movement that was neither wholly monastic nor wholly popular. Their religious concerns overlapped: both were devoted to collecting and venerating relics, to restoring the purity of Shakyamuni's day that such relics signified, and to aiding the salvation of all creatures. The genius of the Nara revival lies in people like Jōkei, who wrote scholarly treatises on Hossō doctrine, and in people like Chōgen, who designed temples and sometimes built them with their own hands.

Each inherited a long tradition of religious withdrawal—one became a recluse, the other began as a wanderer—that lent them the charisma and flexibility of muen status and implicitly criticized current monastic practice. Their power derived in part from marginality or outsiderhood, a phenomenon that Victor Turner has described as "the power of the weak" (1974:234–235). In Turner's analysis, those ouside, on the margins of, or at the bottom of social structure can claim special power, often residing in a magical, ritual, or moral status that transcends their structural weakness. In medieval Japan, such powers were inherent in the marginal status of recluses like Jōkei and onetime wanderers like Chōgen. Within the Buddhist tradition, for example, the recluse in his insubstantial dwelling acted out the central concept of *mujō*, or the impermanence of all phenomena (see LaFleur 1983:60–79). As Michele Marra has pointed out in his study of the recluse literatus Kamo no Chōmei (1153–1216), withdrawal could provide the opportunity for political attacks on all segments of society, including the elite (1991:70–100); countless other hermits and vagabonds implicitly criticized society simply by choosing to occupy a position on or outside its boundaries.

For Chōgen and Jōkei, this process of empowerment worked in several ways. Jōkei's retirement from Kōfukuji can be interpreted as an abandonment of the private wealth and power that other monks sought in violation of the clerical precepts. In Jōkei's case, withdrawal justified both the moral outrage that underlay his attack on Hōnen and the claim that Kasagidera was an especially pure and sanctified place. It permitted him, moreover, to engage in activities that were quite venal (the pursuit of official rank for the temple, tax exemptions for its shōen, and donations to support its buildings, monks, and services) without arousing suspicion that profits were lining his pockets rather than the temple's coffers. If Ritsu monks in later times were entrusted with such posts as the Tōdaiji daikanjinshiki, it may be because Jōkei and others like him established the honesty and reliability of those who were devoted to the precepts.

Chōgen's power came in part from his life as a muen hijiri prior to his assumption of the Tōdaiji post. His experience as an ascetic wanderer and kanjin hijiri gave him the practical experience as well as the vision to pursue the Tōdaiji project. It permitted him to take an outsider's view of the temple when setting priorities for construction, and thus it was logical to build the pagoda before the lecture hall and monks' residence; whereas the latter were designed primarily for the use of the monks themselves, the pagoda, visible from a distance, was built for the public eye. Chōgen's preference for the pagoda can be seen as a criticism of the private concerns that, in his eyes, guided monks' priorities; the sentiments that he stated explicitly in his testament were also expressed in his construction plan. His position as an outsider—as the Visitor deity bringing bounty from afar—validated his emphasis on the temple's public role.

To consider Chōgen and Jōkei only as outsiders, however, ignores their powerful associations with the most exalted figures of Japan's ruling elite. Their achievements came in large part from their ability to manipulate these associations without being totally bound by them. The activities of these two individuals suggest ways in which marginality can shore up structure rather than subvert it, and it is even possible to characterize their kanjin enterprises as reactionary efforts by old, elite temples to defend their fortunes against threats to their domination of Japanese Buddhism.

In the long view, however, this relationship between margin and center contained elements of subversion that are not immediately apparent. It is true that Chōgen and Jōkei both contributed to the maintenance and expansion of temple power, and this enterprise may be seen as reactionary in its results if not in its intent. Even as other branches of Japan's aristocratic establishment were weakening in the face of the warrior challenge, temples gained strength as they adjusted, both financially and ideologically, to the new age. Yet, as I will demonstrate in the next chapter, this adjustment, which required that temples forge new alliances and develop new approaches to secure patrons, helped to transform Japanese Buddhism into a religion for people in all social classes and one that was not always allied with the powerful against the powerless. The process begun by Jōkei and Chōgen was continued by men such as Eizon and his followers, who used kanjin campaigns to involve temples in secular life at the local level and thus brought Buddhism even closer to the people.

Five

BUILDING BRIDGES AND SAVING SOULS

In the Kamakura period, the diffusion of wealth and power into provincial hands provided religious institutions with new problems and new possibilities. Even large temples could no longer rely on their status as members of the central elite, but found it necessary to create ties with the same local magnates and communities that were threatening that elite's monopoly on power. In this chapter, I will examine the way kanjin campaigns were used to establish these ties, with special attention to the following questions: the relative values of persuasion and of coercion in extracting donations; the services that temples and kanjin hijiri performed on behalf of the lay community; and the way in which kanjin activity helped to form collectivities based not on status and hierarchy, but instead on the ties of communitas.

Scholars sometimes point to the decline of the shōen system as one reason why temples turned increasingly to kanjin in the Kamakura age. From the viewpoint of the proprietary class, to which large temples and shrines belonged, it may in fact have seemed that the system was breaking down. On the contrary, it was healthy enough to support the warrior government at Kamakura and its local representatives, the jitō; and despite widespread concern, it would continue to maintain the aristocracy comfortably for many years to come. But the main beneficiaries of the shōen system were beginning to change: many proprietors no longer received the same proportion of income from their lands that they had in the Heian period. When jitō were inserted into the hierarchy of claims to income from the land, proprietors lost part of their share. In addition, local magnates and small holders had learned how to manipulate the system to their own benefit. As absentee landlords, proprietors had always found it difficult to manage distant shōen and to guarantee themselves adequate receipts. When central controls began to falter in the mid-Kamakura period, proprietors could not even be sure that local managers would send them the agreed percentage of the yield. For some time, moreover, local society had been growing more prosperous, as small-scale land reclamation projects stabilized agriculture and increased production. This prosperity benefited local magnates, especially those who held shōen management posts or dealt with financial matters or the transport of goods (Harrington 1982:227–228). It was often these notables, many of whom were bushi and thus had military power, who infringed upon the proprietors' share of income, threatening the financial health of large temples. But such developments also fostered new religious institutions and encouraged existing ones to seek support from these same local magnates. Powerful bushi founded their own family temples, or *ujidera*. Other temples were established by prosperous commoners, who pooled their resources to restore abandoned temples or build new ones, a process that began in advanced regions of the Kinai in the twelfth century and in more remote locations in the thirteenth (Tanaka 1984:5–6). Like the shōen, the Buddhist establishment was not in eclipse but in a process of transformation, and this process strengthened its ties with new holders of power.

When temples turned increasingly to kanjin campaigns in the middle of the thirteenth century, the competition for donations became severe. On two separate occasions, Nara monks complained that kanjin hijiri from other temples had saturated their neighborhood, jamming their own message and obstructing their fundraising efforts. To gain an edge in this competitive situation, temples devised a variety of kanjin methods, any or all of which might be used by a single institution. Sometimes temples obtained authorization from the court or the bakufu to extract taxes and tolls from the public, thinly disguising the coercive nature of these levies by calling them kanjin. At other times, temples developed innovative ways to attract voluntary contributions, such as selling amulets or charging fees to view relics and hear sermons. Perhaps the most potent method, however, used the paradigm of Gyōki as a public works engineer. By performing tasks that had great value to the community, temples won themselves positions of power in the local social structure. Much of this work fell to kanjin hijiri, who collected donations for bridges as well as temples, dispensed charity to the poor, and even buried the dead. Ritsu temples, monks, and affiliated hijiri took a prominent part in all these kanjin efforts. Respected at every level of lay society for their devotion to the precepts, these central actors in the Nara revival were the ideal figures to win public confidence and extend the influence of Buddhist institutions and teachings. The history of kanjin campaigns in the Kamakura period, especially from the mid-thirteenth century onward, also becomes a history of Ritsu monks and institutions and the way that they interacted with the lay public—in short, the history of the Nara revival at work in the world.

Taxes, Tolls, and the Institutionalization of Kanjin Campaigns

In his miscellany *Shasekishū* (Sand and Pebbles, completed in 1283), the Zen monk Mujū Ichien recounts the construction of the pagoda at the Kamakura temple Kenninji. The task was accomplished by the widow of the Genji general Kajiwara Kagetoki, who sold three parcels of land and donated the proceeds to support the project. The pagoda was built, according to Mujū, "without the least inconvenience to anyone." The other temple buildings, however, were continually destroyed by fire, a phenomenon that Mujū attributes to cosmic retribution for the improper means of their financing: ". . . were [the fires] not because [the temple] was brought to completion with such fraudulent 'donations' as taxes levied on people's houses? And was this not contrary to the wishes of the Buddha?" (Morrell 1985:230–232; Mujū 1966:362–364 [book 8, no. 23]). In this passage Mujū identifies and criticizes an increasingly common practice of the middle and late Kamakura periods: special taxes and tolls levied for the benefit of temples and subsumed under the name kanjin.

Coercive kanjin usually took one of two forms. One was the *munebechi sen*, a flat tax imposed on each household within a given area, usually a province or two but sometimes the entire nation. Second, certain temples obtained the permission of court and bakufu to erect toll barriers along public highways or to charge fees for shipments unloaded at certain ports. Evidence of these levies begins to appear in documents of the middle Kamakura period. Even earlier, however, the voluntary nature of kanjin campaigns can be called into question. Both the Kasagidera requests and the imperial edict authorizing the Tōdaiji campaign stipulated that donations not be forced from the people. The mention of coercion suggests that it sometimes took place, on the part of either powerful temples or zealous individual hijiri. Nevertheless, prior to the 1250s most kanjin efforts appeared to be voluntary.

The use of the term *kanjin* to denote a levy was an ironic twist in the history of temple funding. When temples sought voluntary donations to kanjin campaigns in the Heian period, it was largely in order to supplement income extracted from other sources. Most temples had some shōen holdings, and many large temples were government-sponsored institutions with a claim on tax revenue. Temples turned to kanjin in part because these sources had become unsatisfactory, but as long as kanjin campaigns were ad hoc efforts devised to fund specific projects, their proceeds were unpredictable and often insufficient. Though the search for willing donations had great religious and political value, many temples succumbed to the temptation to regularize this source of income, too, by making it into a tax.

This development was a natural outgrowth of the institutionalization of kanjin campaigns and the assumption of quasi-public functions by kanjin hijiri. The seeds were sown when the government initiated the Tōdaiji campaign. In the view of Nagamura Makoto, the government's action gave public recognition to an activity originally carried out privately among the people (1981:64). Through granting the daikanjinshiki, a post beyond the control of the temple monks' assembly, the state appropriated kanjin methods for its own ends. Political leaders intent on using kanjin for their own purposes sometimes even forced their followers to donate to campaigns, as when Yoritomo demanded that his vassals support kanjin efforts for Tōdaiji and Zenkōji. Conversely, once kanjin campaigns had received state sanction in this fashion, temples were able to appropriate state authority to back their requests, turning them into demands.

There may be yet another reason why temples began to rely on state authority: to seek protection against predatory officials and local warriors who interfered with kanjin campaigns. This problem plagued even powerful temples such as Kōfukuji, which virtually controlled Yamato province.   In their efforts to finance the reconstruction of the Hokuendō, one of the buildings destroyed in the conflagration of 1180, temple monks launched a kanjin campaign but had to admonish officials of one Yamato district not to obstruct the collection of donations.

Two documents recount the effort, initiated in 1207: one is a kanjin request, and the second is a *kudashibumi* (order) from the Kōfukuji *mandokoro* (temple office) to officials of Shikinoshimo district. The first document describes the Hokuendō of yore, lists its contents, details its distinguished history, claims a minor miracle for the image of Miroku within, and laments the disaster of the fire. "We temple monks shall muster our resources," the kanjin solicitor writes, "and travel near and far, appealing to the faithful of Yamato province" (Sōshō 1960:244; Takeuchi 1971–1991, 3:326 [doc. 1694]). The request suggests that donors will form ties with the Buddha that will enable them to obtain salvation in the Tosotsu heaven. The resemblance to the Kasagidera requests is not surprising, since Jōkei was involved in the kanjin effort and may have written this document (Yasuda 1983:68–69). In any case, the request indicates a kanjin campaign of the voluntary type, similar to the Kasagidera efforts.

The kudashibumi was issued to officials of a district where Kōfukuji had a number of shōen but was by no means the only holder. The order stipulated that officials cooperate with the kanjin effort (Sōshō 1960:245; Takeuchi 1971–1991, 3:325 [doc. 1693]). Both the kanjin request and this document made it clear that donations would not be forced from the people; the kanjin request was couched in persuasive language, and the kudashibumi stated explicitly that reluctant givers would not be chastised. The only people being forced to do anything in this case were the district officials, who had to make sure the kanjin proceeds were forwarded to the temple and not, presumably, diverted to their own pockets.

Somewhat later in the period, the question of coercion becomes more problematic. For example, it seems that the Nara temple Tōshōdaiji initially favored a voluntary campaign but turned eventually to coercive methods. Tōshōdaiji's story begins in 1255, when it requested permission to exhibit relics it owned on Kōfukuji territory (Takeuchi 1971–1991, 11:88 [doc. 7886]; Hosokawa 1987:25–26). The intention was to display the relics in order to attract potential donors. Tōshōdaiji complained that Yamato province was saturated with kanjin hijiri, to the extent that donors could not distinguish between charlatans and honest solicitors. Thus the Tōshōdaiji monks sought the prestige of their powerful neighbor to avoid confusion with disreputable hijiri from other temples swarming the countryside.

At this point the campaign appears to have been a voluntary one that successfully attracted numerous gifts both large and small. The stated purpose of the effort was the general repair and reconstruction of dilapidated buildings and images. In 1256 the temple issued a circular in the form of a woodblock print, decorated with the picture of a buddha and requesting donations of one shō of rice per person to repair the image of Shakyamuni in the temple's Golden Hall (Ishida 1964:137). This request was probably only one of many for similar projects.

Donation records of 1258 found inside an image of Sha-kyamuni (perhaps the one in the Golden Hall) suggest the strong appeal of kanjin campaigns (Takeuchi 1971-1991, 11:273-284 [docs. 8221-8249]). All of the donors listed in these records displayed their devotion to Shakyamuni by reciting the nenbutsu in his name. In addition, some offered substantial gifts, such as two or three thousand rolls of cloth. The many donors who are listed only by name probably gave very small offerings. Donors came from a wide social and economic spectrum, including professional clergy, lay believers who had retired from active life and had taken religious names, local elites (those listed by surname), and common folk (listed only by given names, such as Tarō and Jirō). The suffix *onna* after many names indicates that a substantial number of donors were women. Some donors had adopted the *amida* suffix, which by this time had become a fairly common appellation among lay Buddhists.

Although the display of relics apparently attracted many donations, it does not seem that they were substantial enough to satisfy the temple, which then chose to pursue other methods. In 1258 the head of the Fujiwara family, which oversaw Kōfukuji affairs, granted Tōshōdaiji permission to collect one shō of rice per household from Kōfukuji holdings (Takeuchi 1971-1991, 11:291 [doc. 8271], 308-309 [doc. 8308]). The assessment was still under way in 1260, when two of Kōfukuji's subtemples, Daijōin and Ichijōin, ordered their shōen to comply with the 1258 edict

(Takeuchi 1971–1991, 12:17 [doc. 8553], 12:20 [doc. 8560]). The Tōshōdaiji effort, in short, combined both voluntary and coercive kanjin methods. Although voluntary methods were more suitable for attracting converts in accord with the temple's religious mission, kanjin as tax no doubt turned the better profit. By the 1250s many temples had obtained permission to collect tolls along highways and at ports. In 1256, for example, the right to conduct kanjin tolls at Akashi port in Harima province was granted to Tamonji, and in 1261 a fee of ten mon was assessed each boat proceeding to Kyōto through the port of Yodo and assigned to the repair of Kongosan Naigein (Amino 1974:290). Even the most important temples sometimes turned to this method. In 1282, for instance, the court authorized Tōji to assess each household in the country a ten-mon munebechi sen for building reconstruction (Amino 1978a:197).

Though toll barriers were often erected at places traditionally under the emperor's control, such as *mikuriya* (tribute fields) or imperial hunting and falconry grounds (Amino 1974:290), two examples from 1310 indicate that "kanjin" levies could be ordered by either court or bakufu: Kogawadera Seidōin in Kii province received permission from the court to levy a munebechi sen of ten kan in Yamashiro, Kawachi, Izumi, Settsu, Harima, and Kii provinces (Takeuchi 1971–1991, 31:233 [doc. 23893], 388 [doc. 24281]), an authorization ratified the next year by the bakufu deputy at Rokuhara in Kyōto; and Kamakura ordered a munebechi sen in Shinano province in 1310 for reconstruction at Taizenji in Kai (Takeuchi 1971–1991, 31:270 [doc. 23984]). Seidōin had already attempted a voluntary kanjin campaign but had failed to raise sufficient revenue for its building project. For this temple and perhaps others, voluntary kanjin was the method of first choice, and monks may have resorted to the munebechi sen only when shortfalls compelled them to do so.

Mujū was not alone in raising objections to such heavy-handed methods. In 1291, in a series of documents related to holdings of the Kōya temple complex in Kii, shōen officials pledged not to use kanjin as a pretext for demanding payments from cultivators (Takeuchi 1971–1991, 23:134–142 [docs. 17683–17684, 17686–17687]). Mujū had complained on religious grounds, but other objections probably rested on economic and political considerations. When Kōfukuji's subtemple Daijōin assessed a munebechi sen in Yamato province in 1300, it was necessary to apologize to the holders of estates other than Kōfukuji shōen, promising that the levy was a one-time-only intrusion on their tax-exempt status (Takeuchi 1971–1991, 27:203–204 [doc. 20539]). This was not the first time that Kōfukuji had encroached on the rights of others, however; in 1277, for example, Tōdaiji complained that its estates had been forced to provide laborers to assist in Kōfukuji construction (Yasuda 1983:69). Coercive kanjin, in other words, not only burdened the ordinary taxpayer, it violated the territory of other proprietors.

Such methods gave kanjin a bad name and seem to have generated efforts to distinguish voluntary from coercive campaigns. Increasingly in the middle and late Kamakura period, voluntary efforts were designated as such by terms such as "halfpenny, scrap of wood" kanjin (see, for example, Takeuchi 1971–1991, 28:352 [doc. 21869]). Despite the common use of coercive methods, many small projects seem to have been funded through voluntary donations. For example, a bell at Kinpusen in Satsuma province cast in 1311 was financed by the faithful of "the ten directions" (Takeuchi 1971–1991, 32:89 [doc. 24482]). In the next year, donations were collected to thatch the roof of Tamawakasu shrine in Oki province. Hijiri dunned passersby on the road in front of the shrine (Takeuchi 1971–1991, 32:179 [doc. 24649]), much as the Chinkōji hijiri had almost three hundred years before.

Small donors continued to be targets for kanjin campaigns, such as the one conducted in 1280 for Kumetaji (Takeuchi 1971–1991, 18:349–350 [doc. 13946]) and that in 1319 for the repair of the pagoda roof at Myōtsūji in Wakasa (Takeuchi 1971–1991, 36:3 [doc. 27532]). Kanjin requests for both of these efforts specifically mention *shomin* or *jinmin* (commoners) as part of their intended audience. Small donors sometimes formed kechienshu such as the one composed of 108 faithful listed on a plaque dated 1322 at Kumano shrine in Sado (Takeuchi 1971–1991, 36:256 [doc. 28134]).

The thirteenth-century collection *Shasekishū* contains stories in which preachers sought contributions from very humble donors. In one tale, a preacher officiated at services for fishermen at Lake Biwa in Ōtsu province (Mujū 1966:266–267; Morrell 1985: 187 [book 6, no. 6]). In order to attract donations, the preacher had to distort Buddhist doctrine, which criticized those such as fishermen who lived by taking life. He claimed that the lake was the eye of the Chinese T'ien-t'ai master Chih I and that removing fish from the lake was equivalent to removing dust from a buddha's eye. The fishermen donated generously, won over by this application of the doctrine of expedient means. Gifts from the common folk might not always have been desirable, however: in another tale from *Shasekishū,* when a Yamato preacher delivered a sermon at a woodcutter's home, he received nothing but a bundle of dried taro stalks (Mujū 1966:264–265; Morrell 1985:185 [book 6, no. 4]). While gifts such as this were just what Shōmu and Chōgen had seemed to want when requesting twigs, grass, or clumps of earth, they were probably not of much use to the preacher's temple.

The proliferation of kanjin campaigns seems to have inspired innovative means to attract contributions. Two of these methods, distributing amulets and charging admission to hear sermons and to view temple treasures and engi, seem particularly suited to the small donor, although some were inspired to give substantial amounts.

The amulet method can be traced back to Chōgen, whose *Namuamidabutsu sazenshū* lists more than one thousand *inbutsu* (stamped buddha-images) among the items at Jōdodō, his kanjin base at Tōdaiji, and at the Watanabe bessho (Chōgen 1934:44–45; Nakanodō 1978:18–19). Chōgen probably distributed these to donors as amulets, conferring the *amida* suffix at the same time. Later in the Kamakura period, amulet peddling became fairly common; perhaps the best-known examples come from the kanjin efforts of Gokurakubō at Gangōji in Nara, documented by extensive archaeological research led by Gorai Shigeru (1964). Another example is the campaign to reconstruct the irrigation pond at Kumetaji in Izumi province. In a request issued in 1289, Kumetaji's chief monk Zenni sought donations to have sixty thousand stupas made: "With these stupas we will repair the embankments of our temple's pond" (Takeuchi 1971–1991, 22:197–198 [doc. 16906]). In other words, the temple first sought help from wealthy or devoted patrons to have small wooden plaques or woodblock prints manufactured as amulets and then sold the amulets to finance the reconstruction project. The Pure Land master Ippen also distributed amulets, describing his act as kanjin and claiming that the amulets signified that the recipient had already attained salvation (Foard 1977:147). The amulets may have been exchanged for contributions, although there is no direct evidence that that was the case.

Another method of attracting donations was to charge admission to those who wished to view—and venerate—the temple's images and other treasures (Nakanodō 1978:27–30). Sometimes viewers were admitted to the temple, and sometimes the treasures themselves were taken "on tour" as in the case of Tōshōdaiji's relics. This method apparently attracted a wide spectrum of donors: when Kachiodera, a Settsu province temple, exhibited its images of Yakushi and Kannon in Kyōto, it chose two separate venues, the Nijō Higashitōin Jizōdō, in a neighborhood of aristocrats and officials, and Shijō Takakura Shakadō, near the homes of artisans and merchants. The exhibits netted more than two hundred kan, which would have been enough, for instance, to cast seven bronze bells (Nakanodō 1978:29).

The exhibitions of relics initiated a chain of events in which pictures and dance performances were employed to secure the temple even more donations (Nakanodō 1978:29–30). The temple first reinvested ten kan from its exhibit receipts to have illustrations made for its engi. In one standard kanjin method that became especially popular in the Muromachi period, etoki-hōshi (picture-explaining monks) used illustrated engi as props for storytelling. Kachiodera probably displayed its engi in this way in 1248, inspiring at least one wealthy woman to make a donation to support public readings of the Hannya sūtra. The same temple also sponsored bugaku (dance) performances, using the receipts for temple projects.

Some scholars have argued that, because it was used so often, the coercive kanjin method became the norm in the Kamakura period (Nakanodō 1978:20–23; Yasuda 1983:67). Indeed, important temples seemed to favor coercion, and the lion's share of "kanjin" receipts may have come from tolls and taxes. Yet voluntary campaigns remained important to smaller temples, if only because they lacked the political influence to generate a mune-bechi sen. Moreover, temples that relied too heavily on coercive methods had to endure public disapproval. The use of the term kanjin to disguise taxes and tolls for religious purposes suggests that the concept of voluntary giving was still a useful construct, even when it masked coercive reality in a very imperfect manner.

Of course, some of the innovative kanjin methods developed in the Kamakura period were clearly based on persuasion rather than coercion. The people who flocked to view relics or to hear the explanations of the etoki-hōshi formed a willing audience; if they were drawn as much by curiosity and the wish to be entertained as by the desire for salvation, they were no doubt treated to a healthy dose of preaching. The use of dance, theater, and pictures was also a type of evangelism, since the themes illustrated were religious ones expected to entice the audience onto the road to salvation. Thus kanjin efforts continued to be an important vehicle for the spread of Buddhist teachings.

Eizon, Ritsu Monks, and Kanjin Campaigns

In the middle and late Kamakura period, Ritsu monks assumed a prominent role in kanjin efforts, both voluntary campaigns and the collection of tolls and taxes. They sought donations to support their own temples and were often chosen for daikanjin positions at temples to which they did not belong. After 1292, for instance, "Zenritsu" monks—who combined Zen practices with devotion to the precepts—were regularly appointed to the Tōdaiji daikanjin-shiki. These appointments have been attributed to the perception that these monks were honest, reliable, and free of court and bakufu dominance or factional attachments (Nagamura 1981:81, 88). Another reason, perhaps, was that kanjin solicitors were often put in charge of construction projects, not only temples but also bridges, roads, and irrigation systems; and the labor for these projects was frequently provided by the outcast hinin, with whom Ritsu monks had close ties. Ritsu monks affiliated with Saidaiji in Nara were particularly active in kanjin campaigns, public works projects, and charitable activities.

The founder of the Saidaiji Ritsu lineage was Eizon (1201–1290). Born into a rural family, he suffered the death of his mother at an early age, and his father, too poor to care for his children, sent the boy to be raised in another home.[1] The boy was shuttled from one foster home to another but was finally taken in by a monk at the Shingon temple Daigoji, for whom he performed simple religious tasks. After some hesitancy, Eizon decided to study Shingon esoteric teachings, convinced by a mentor that they were the most suitable doctrines for an ordinary person in the age of mappō. He took the tonsure in 1217 and spent most of the next two decades in esoteric practice, traveling on at least one occasion to the Shingon center at Mt. Kōya. In 1234, however, he developed an interest in the monastic precepts, and the next year he moved to Saidaiji. There he spent the remainder of his life, using the temple as a base to restore both the precepts and Buddhism's physical framework of images and temple buildings.

The axes of Eizon's religious life were the precepts and charity, and he combined them in a way that typified the response of Nara-revival monks to the challenge of mappō. In 1236 he and three other men revived an abandoned practice by receiving, in a ceremony at Tōdaiji, the 250 precepts that regulated monastic life. In the absence of an appropriate master, the four administered the precepts to themselves. In so doing, Eizon and his companions simultaneously returned to tradition—by demanding of themselves the upright behavior that most monks had abandoned—and departed from it, taking authority for themselves rather than receiving it from others. Subsequently, Eizon administered the precepts to monks and lay believers (including hinin); the latter were usually given the less restrictive bodhisattva precepts. Eizon also performed numerous acts of charity and public service. He dispensed food and clothing to hinin, preached to them, and steered them toward publicly acceptable behavior. Citing the Buddhist prohibition against taking any life, he fought to protect fish and birds from being killed. Like monks at other important temples, he recited prayers and read sūtras in a campaign to ward off the Mongol invaders who threatened Japan's shores; and he was credited, along with others, for the seemingly miraculous typhoon that wiped out the Mongol fleet in 1281.

Though Eizon attracted attention from important warrior circles—including the Hōjō regents to the military government at Kamakura—he refused their financial support, declaring, "I despise things that are attached to the world and prefer those that are unattached (muen). This is the expedient means (hōben) to preserve the Buddhist law" (Wajima 1959:55). Thus Eizon not only defined the concept of muen as independence from political authorities, he also linked it to the welfare of Buddhism and its institutions. At the same time, he justified his muen status by the doctrine of hōben, which was often used to recommend compromise of various types.

One way to achieve such independence was by relying on the

small gifts of many donors. A list of Saidaiji holdings compiled in 1298 includes many commendations of small plots of land only a few tan in area; most of the donors were local holders in Yamato province (Takeuchi 1971–1991, 26:231–260 [doc. 19893]). Such gifts enabled Eizon to construct a monks' hall in 1247 and a Butsuden in 1249 (Wajima 1959:29). When Eizon dispensed food to hinin in 1267 and again in 1269, he turned to kanjin campaigns to support the effort, and his restoration of the Kawachi temple Kyōkōji was also funded through kanjin means (Wajima 1959:57–60). Active kanjin campaigns had their drawbacks for Eizon, however, as indicated by an incident recorded in *Kongōbusshi Eizon kanshin gakushōki,* thought to be Eizon's own work. In 1255 Eizon decided to have an image of Monju bodhisattva made and installed at Hannyaji, a temple on the outskirts of Nara:

> I had this image carved in order to make it the focus of reverence for all living beings. Originally I intended to conduct a kanjin campaign among rich and poor, and use their donations to obtain materials for the image. However, the city and the countryside have become saturated with those seeking alms from the faithful. Since kanjin has become commonplace, it will not necessarily arouse the deep faith [that inspires donations]. Therefore we did not circulate kanjin appeals but have instead relied on spontaneous contributions. (Nara Kokuritsu Bunkazai Kenkyūjo 1977:34)

The image was dedicated in 1269 to the salvation of the hinin who lived nearby. More than six thousand people, half of them hinin, attended the service in which food and clothing, collected by Eizon's kanjin hijiri disciples, were distributed to the poor (*Hōryūji bettō shidai,* quoted in Wajima 1959:58).

If Eizon did not send his followers from house to house to seek donations for the Monju image, he nevertheless got the word out somehow: according to his disciple Shinkū, "Clergy and laity, and men and women developed believing hearts and donated cloth or a bowl, a scrap of paper, or half a penny" (Takeuchi 1971–1991, 21:256–257 [doc. 16245]). The spontaneous donations probably came from the same local holders who had been sustaining Saidaiji itself with gifts of small plots of land. In other words, Eizon already had a powerful base of support within the community that he could tap for additional projects. If he did not recommend a kanjin campaign at this point, it may have been because that base had already been established in previous campaigns. One reason for this support, no doubt, was the practical benefit of Eizon's undertakings. When Eizon gave alms and preached virtue to the hinin, he was helping to contain a potentially disruptive force. He gave them work on construction projects (Miura 1978:9–10), and in 1275, when he dispensed rice to some three thousand of them, he extracted from their leader a pledge to end antisocial practices such as extortionate begging (Wajima 1959: 77–79). In bringing the hinin under control and directing their efforts toward socially useful undertakings, Eizon no doubt earned the gratitude of both lay authorities and private parties, and enhanced Saidaiji's status and economic power.

Kanjin, Death, and Pollution

The power of monks and temples was based ultimately on the central task undertaken by Buddhist institutions on behalf of the lay population: the management of death. Buddhist teachings explained death, prepared individuals and their families for it, and neutralized the fears of malevolent ghosts and death-induced pollution. Monks and temple affiliates performed funeral rites and buried the dead or their ashes in temple graveyards. Since these services rarely came for free, temples found a major source of financial support in people anxious to ensure that their loved ones escape hell and attain paradise. Prayers and rituals on behalf of the dead were thought crucial to this aim, and temples were guaranteed a steady stream of donations from the family of the deceased. Since mortuary rites were scheduled at set intervals for many years after an individual's death, families and temples formed long-term ties that might last for generations.

It was no doubt such families that contributed most readily to campaigns for temple building projects. Kanjin records contain ample evidence of gifts on behalf of the dead. For instance, some who donated to Gangōji Gokurakubō in the 1260s did so in memory of a "beloved father" or a "lamented mother" (Takeuchi 1971–1991, 13:375–385 [docs. 9919–10234]). In 1325, when a woman donated ten koku of rice for the copying of the Lotus sūtra at Myōtsūji in Wakasa province, she made this typical declaration: "My purpose in making this donation is my parents' salvation, my own rebirth in the Gokuraku paradise, and the distribution of spiritual benefits equally to everyone in the world" (Takeuchi 1971–1991, 38:29 [doc. 29277]). Families were motivated in part by the fear that the abandoned dead would become ghosts to torment the living. Buddhism offered an ideal method to treat both this fear and the genuine concern that people must have felt for their dead loved ones. Directed to paradise by rituals and prayers, the dead were both saved and rendered harmless. Such elements were central to the Chinese Buddhist practice on which Japanese mortuary rituals were based. Stephen F. Teiser has examined the history of the ghost festival in China (Yü-lan-p'en; Japan's Obon), in which people made offerings to Buddhist monks, thus helping "to effect the passage of the dead from the status of a recently deceased, threatening ghost to that of a stable, pure and venerated ancestor" (1988:13). Transforming the dead in this way was one purpose of the annual ghost festival as it was practiced in Japan, of mortuary rituals independent of the season, and of countless donations to kanjin campaigns in memory of the dead.

The ability to guide the dead to salvation gave an awesome responsibility to the living and extraordinary power to the monks on whom the faithful depended. As Teiser suggests in the case of China, the ties between religious specialists and family were strengthened, as monks became "an essential party in the cycle of exchange linking ancestors and descendants" (1988:196–197). Jacques Le Goff has pointed out a similar phenomenon in medieval Europe (1984:12). When purgatory was invented as a temporary dwelling place that one might escape after suffering punishment, the living were given the opportunity to intercede for the dead through prayer: "What an enhancement of the power of the living there was in this hold over the dead! Meanwhile, here below, the extension of communal ties into the other world enhanced the solidarity of families, religious organizations, and confraternities. And for the Church, what a marvelous instrument of power!"

The ability of the living to save the dead through prayers, be they Buddhist rites or masses for Christian sinners, had significant results for the medieval religious community as well as for the families of the dead. Buddhist and Christian institutions alike obtained a new position of power through the ability to extract offerings and devotion from a dead soul's living family.

In both Japan and medieval Europe, religious institutions adjusted mortuary belief and practice in accordance with the growing complexities of society. The crucial factor in both instances was the development of a middle class that needed religious validation for a way of life that was viewed as wicked or was at best ignored in existing religious schemes. Le Goff has argued that the creation of purgatory represents the adjustment of sacred geography to the emergence of social categories between the old dichotomies of rich and poor, and clergy and laity (1984:7). Purgatory gave hope to those of intermediate virtue: people who were neither good enough to merit heaven nor bad enough to deserve eternal damnation. That the circle of the intermediate was expanded to include even usurers (Le Goff 1984:305) suggests that "intermediacy" was defined in part by society's economic needs. Usurers violated the laws of the church against lending with interest and thus were despised as sinners, yet they were crucial to economic growth. More generally speaking, the church looked askance at merchants, whose pursuit of profit seemed improper or even sinful (Little 1978:35–41). Thus the creation of purgatory as a place that might accommodate such "sinners" answered the needs of the commercializing economy of the twelfth and thirteenth centuries.

The Japanese counterpart of the medieval European usurer or merchant was doubtless the warrior, who took life in defiance of Buddhist precepts. However, Buddhism offered various avenues toward salvation for the warrior class, including prayers for relatives dead in battle, the slain enemy, or oneself in the face of death. Thus people had memorial stupas and markers erected for those who had died in battle, and temples housed registers with names of the war dead.

When civil warfare in 1333 brought an end to the Kamakura bakufu, such concerns must have become particularly compelling. In that year a memorial tablet was erected at a Musashi province temple in memory of a warrior who had died in battle at the age of twenty-six (Takeuchi 1971–1991, 41:268 [doc. 32175]). A kanjin hijiri's name appears on the tablet, suggesting that the warrior's grieving family donated to the temple at the time. A *kakochō* (death registry) kept at a temple in Ōmi province lists warriors who were killed or forced to commit suicide in a battle in Kyōto fought in the same year (Takeuchi 1971–1991, 41:252–258 [doc. 32137]). Though no special prayers for salvation were appended to the registry, the kakochō form was derived from kanjin records, in which living donors added the names of the dead in order to effect their rebirth in paradise. Gifts to temples served as tangible evidence of the sincerity of surviving relatives and must have encouraged monks to offer extra prayers on behalf of the petitioners and their dead.

The rites of death gave the Buddhist clergy the opportunity to serve the needs of the bushi, tapping their fears and desires, and bolstering the structures that they used to claim power. Buddhist mortuary rituals and the memorial markers in temple graveyards emphasized the patrilineage *(ie)* and thus enhanced the family cohesion of local warrior magnates, helping them to extend their power over followers and territory. Like ancestral rites in more modern times, mortuary rites were useful in preserving the awareness of the ie as a corporate body that transcended the generations. Stupas and steles often commemorated these rites, especially in eastern Japan, and their placement and inscriptions suggest that most of them were erected by bushi families (Tsuruoka 1967:67–68).

Mortuary ritual also helped Buddhist specialists to establish themselves in rural communities. Led by kanjin hijiri, villages formed confraternities to sponsor collective mortuary rites. In 1299, for example, the kanjin hijiri Gen'a formed a kechienshu of 120 people to support nenbutsu services that lasted for a thousand days (Kawakatsu 1971:60), commemorating the act by a stupa erected at the graveyard of Mt. Kōya. Actions of this sort must have contributed to communal solidarity, binding neighbor to neighbor and everyone to the dead. Nor were the poor ignored. For example, under Eizon's leadership, Ritsu monks restored and managed the common graveyards at temples such as Sairinji and Kyōkōji in Kawachi province (Hosokawa 1987:83–90). Such services were invaluable to the poor, who previously had been forced to abandon corpses or to bury them in shallow unmarked graves.

In medieval Japan, moreover, mortuary rituals were not even limited to the dead. Encouraged by kanjin hijiri, people formed kechienshu that held *gyakushu*, pre-death "funerals" on behalf of their living participants. In 1296, for example, a kanjin hijiri collected donations from more than one hundred people in Musashi province to hold a gyakushu. They commemorated the event with a stone tablet inscribed as follows: "We pray that [the benefits of] this meritorious act will disseminate widely to everyone and that we and all others shall embark together upon the road to buddhahood" (Kawakatsu 1978:110). Gyakushu usually replicated the complex of memorial ceremonies that followed a person's death—sometimes conflating them into a single grand service—and were thought especially efficacious for assuring a good afterlife (Kawakatsu 1972:149). In this way, temples found additional opportunities to provide mortuary services and to expand both profits and influence thereby.

Although monks of all affiliations participated in funeral services, associates of Ritsu temples played an especially prominent role in the Kamakura period. This activity was not without problems, since contact with corpses was thought to transmit ritual pollution, and generally speaking those who handled corpses were treated as outcasts. Ritsu monks, however, were highly respected by all segments of society, including the court aristocracy and the bushi elite; this respect was a crucial element in maintaining the influence and financial health of Ritsu institutions. Hosokawa Ryōichi argues that the monks buffered themselves against pollution and maintained their prestigious social standing by using lower-class affiliates called *saikaishū* to dispose of corpses (1987:9–20). Like muen hijiri, the saikaishū also personally collected donations for kanjin campaigns. Their association with families of the dead, already grateful for services that the temple had provided, was no doubt useful in inspiring contributions.

Saikaishū served the Ritsu temples Saidaiji, Kairyūōji, and Tōshōdaiji, as well as Tōdaiji. Saikaishū were distinguished from regular monks in various ways. For example, they were not allowed to bathe with the regular monks at Kairyūōji, according to records of 1347; they could, however, use the same utensils. Moreover, saikaishū were not expected to keep the entire set of monastic precepts. In fact, they may have been lay brothers, and in any case, they were not thought to be as "pure" as regular Ritsu monks. However, it does not seem that they were regarded as hinin, even though they probably performed similarly "unclean" tasks. Some of them were local peasants, such as the man whose kanjin efforts for Tōshōdaiji in 1316 were noted as particularly effective in his home village, a nearby farming community (Hosokawa 1987:24). In short, the saikaishū were not outcasts like the hinin who lived apart from the farming community, but lower-class individuals who performed tasks that regular monks may have found polluting or simply onerous.[2]

However, the question of pollution is a complex one that embraces factors other than corpses and death. For example, Ritsu monks such as Eizon dealt directly with the hinin, and according to the fourteenth-century history *Genkō shakusho* (1913: 297–298), Eizon's disciple Ninshō (1217–1303) transported lepers (considered hinin) by carrying them on his back. Taboos against lepers were fueled by very real fears of contagion; as for other hinin, the fact that they generally lived in their own special ghettos indicates that they were shunned by others who feared "catching" their ritual pollution. Like European saints who licked the sores of lepers, however, Ritsu monks did not allow either fear or disgust to prevent them from helping the unfortunate.

Some Ritsu monks went one step further, even identifying the bodhisattva Monju (and by extension themselves) with the despised hinin. When Eizon's image of Monju was dedicated at Hannyaji, Eizon's disciple Shinkū claimed that several miracles occurred, including appearances of the bodhisattva as a hinin in a parturition hut, perhaps to perform the polluting task of removing the placenta, as a healer giving moxabustion to an invalid, and as a gigantic leper who beat lazy monks (Takeuchi 1971–1991, 21:256–257 [doc. 16245]; Hosokawa 1987:58–60). On the surface Monju takes the form of an outcast, an incarnation justified by the fact that he had appeared as a poor man in the sūtras (Taira 1984:283). But Monju may also represent the Ritsu monks, whose moral uprightness can be seen as a powerful defense against pollution.

In fact, Buddhism offered novel approaches to the problem of pollution, as illustrated by an episode from the Kamakura period Shugendō text *Shozan engi* (Sakurai, Hagiwara, and Miyata 1975:104–108). On a mountain pilgrimage, the sixth-century ascetic En no Gyōja encounters evil spirits and the pollutions of childbirth, the eating of carrion, and death. But he overcomes pollution through a mixture of Shintō rites such as *harae* (purification) and Buddhist rites such as reading sūtras and forming mudrā (gestures thought to effect union with a buddha). The Buddhist component is particularly effective, since Buddhist rituals are employed not only to chase away evil and pollution, but to convert them into their opposites. The evil spirits seem unwillingly bound to malevolence, and they ask En no Gyōja to use his rituals to purify them—or even to make them disappear. In one case, he advises an evil spirit to bathe in a holy river (the Shintō rite of ablutions) in order to attain rebirth at the time of Miroku Buddha's advent. Thus evil and pollution are not only defeated by ritual, but are "saved" in a Buddhist sense.

Shinkū's miracle tale also involves the conversion of pollution, not merely its defeat or neutralization. In the first of the tale's episodes, Monju takes the form of a hinin engaged in a polluting task. The task itself becomes a *bosatsu gyō,* an act that by definition fulfills the bodhisattva's function of helping humankind. The second episode does not specifically cast Monju as a hinin but places him in contact with illness that may be seen as ritually polluting. Again, an act that ordinary persons were probably reluctant to perform becomes a bosatsu gyō. In the third episode, Monju reappears as a hinin, this time with a mission to punish (and thereby reform) lazy monks. Here Monju explicitly performs the task undertaken by Ritsu monks such as Eizon, whose adherence to the precepts implicitly censured their negligent fellows.

If Monju stands in for the Ritsu monk in Shinkū's tale, then the ability of Ritsu monks to confront pollution without apparent damage to themselves becomes easier to understand. Like the evil spirits that endangered En no Gyōja and were sent on their way to salvation, pollution is confronted and made the occasion for a bosatsu gyō. It can also be argued that Ritsu monks and hinin, through their mutual identification with Monju, could be seen as in some sense equivalent, occupying marginal status even though one had withdrawn from society and was honored for it and the other was cast out and despised.

The ability of Ritsu monks and institutions to perform funerals, handle corpses, and deal with hinin allowed them to perform invaluable services for the lay community. In that they fulfilled functions that might otherwise have fallen to the state, Ritsu monks assumed public responsibilities. They benefited public health and sanitation, controlled potential dissidents, and soothed the community psychologically by seeming to protect it from pollution. Their practical services go a long way toward explaining why they were so successful in collecting donations that they were often given kanjin posts at temples that were not their own.

Hijiri and Local Society: Construction Projects

When local magnates and small holders built and supported temples, they expected something in return. Rewards seemed no less real if they were collectible only in one's next life, and donors valued the prospect of rebirth in paradise for themselves or for others of their choosing. Reasons for giving were complex, however, and not all donors were stimulated only by faith or by concern for a loved one's fate after death. If Go Shirakawa could build a temple as a monument to his glory, then local magnates could do the same on a smaller scale. Gifts to temples were public announcements that the donor was both prosperous and pious; more than that, in an age when religious and secular matters were never clearly distinguished, gifts seemed to muster the power of the buddhas on the donor's side. The value of pious connections was clearly demonstrated when local magnates used kanjin hijiri to help them build roads and bridges. Technologically adept and skilled in the management of materials and labor, hijiri could be a valuable resource to local magnates or to entire communities that wanted to use such projects to increase their own wealth and power.

Ritsu monks were also prominent among the kanjin hijiri who helped communities build bridges, roads, hospitals, and leprosariums. Eizon, for example, collected donations for the repair of the Uji bridge in Kyōto in 1281 (Wajima 1959:89). Public works were often justified in religious terms, and kanjin efforts to fund them were hard to distinguish from efforts to fund the construction of temples.

When kanjin hijiri helped with public works projects, they followed the models of Japanese Buddhist saints such as Gyōki, Kūkai, and Kūya, depicted in legends as builders of temples, roads, and bridges, and diggers of irrigation ponds and wells. Moreover, the involvement of hijiri in public works projects was a natural outgrowth of their kanjin activity. The same methods were used to collect donations for a bridge as for a temple; and when kanjin hijiri began to take charge of all phases of temple construction, as did Chōgen, some of the expertise they developed could be applied to secular projects as well.

There are many examples of kanjin efforts to support public works projects in the second half of the Kamakura period. The Zen monk Giin collected donations for the construction of a bridge in Higo province in 1276. Kumetaji's Zenni, an associate of Eizon, repaired his temple's irrigation pond with kanjin donations solicited in 1289. In 1307 Zenni's friend Jissen of Saidaiji joined in a kanjin effort to clear a navigation channel in a river in Bitchū province; at the behest of the bushi proprietor of Hine manor in Izumi province, Jissen also headed a land reclamation project there in 1310. In another example from Izumi province, a document dated 1315 notes that a jitō had appointed a kanjin hijiri to repair the dikes of an irrigation pond that served two villages (Takeuchi 1971-1991, 16:266-267 [doc. 12348, project of 1276]; 22:197-198 [doc. 16906, project of 1289]; 30:161-162 [doc. 23020, project of 1307]; 33:227-228 [doc. 25620, project of 1315]; Miura 1978:5 [project of 1310]). Such activities were sometimes accompanied by the opening of temples, such as Giin's construction of Daijiji at the north end of the bridge.

Sometimes a public works project was initiated by the kanjin hijiri—for example, the Higo bridge; sometimes a local notable secured the help of kanjin hijiri to accomplish a project—for example, the clearing of the Bitchū river; and sometimes a local community sought the help of a kanjin hijiri to restore a local temple, such as Jōdoji in Bingo, completed in 1306. Despite these differences, such projects had two points in common: they required the cooperation of hijiri and the local community, and they were justified in religious terms.

The Higo bridge was constructed through the efforts of Giin (1217-1300), who conducted a kanjin campaign for the project (*Kumamoto ken no chimei* 1985:534; Washio 1966:164-165). According to traditional accounts—which often exalt the backgrounds of religious figures—Giin was the son of an emperor, either Go Toba or Juntoku, and a Fujiwara mother, daughter of the minister of the left. He entered religious life at the Tendai complex on Mt. Hiei and later became a disciple of the Sōtō Zen master Dōgen. Giin traveled twice to China, returning to Japan in 1267 and eventually settling in Higo province. There he obtained the patronage of Kawajiri Yasuaki, whose family had held jitō rights on Kawajiri manor for almost ninety years. Giin is credited with establishing two temples for the benefit of his patrons and personally carving several sacred images.

Kawajiri manor was bounded on the south by the broad mouth of the Midori river. In a document dated 1276, Giin explained the need for a bridge across the river: "People of high and low estate crowd on either bank, bickering constantly. People and horses vie to board small boats that then capsize, drowning their passengers." Vowing to build a bridge to correct the situation, Giin decided to rely on the help of others—in other words, to seek support through a kanjin campaign that sought donations from the "ten directions." He justified his project in religious terms: "When we see a dangerous situation, we must make it safe, [for] the Buddha pities people" (Takeuchi 1971–1991, 16:266–267 [doc. 12348]). The bridge, at Ōwatashi on the manor, was completed in 1278.

The bridge earned Yasuaki's gratitude. In 1282 he donated land at the north end of the bridge so that Giin could build a temple there. The temple, Daijiji, was supported by further donations, including alluvial swampland along Shimabara bay. Giin was charged with draining the land and given the right to exploit it for temple expenses. When Yasuaki's patron Hōjō Tokimune died in 1284, Yasuaki dedicated his gifts to Daijiji to Tokimune's enlightenment. Daijiji and Giin received assistance from the most exalted elements of Japanese society: the retired emperors Go Uda and Fushimi, and the bakufu, which authorized a kanjin effort to repair the bridge in 1299 and supported the temple's right to mobilize labor for the project from the entire province (*Kumamoto ken no chimei* 1985:363, 400, 534–535).

No such exalted names appear in the story of the clearing of the Nariwa river in Bitchū province, but it is another example of cooperation between kanjin hijiri and powerful local patrons. The work was intended to facilitate the transportation of goods, probably iron from northern Bitchū and Bingo (*Okayama ken no chimei* 1988:857).

The project is documented by an inscription carved on a cliff above the river. The brief but revealing legend reads: "Constructing a passage for boats at Kasakami: we began [this section of the project?] on the twentieth day of the seventh month of 1307 and finished on the first of the eighth month. . . . Although the more than ten series of rapids above and below Tatsugashira have made this the most difficult passage in Japan, the bodhisattvas, with their great compassion, pitied us and could not but help us. . . . We sought [contributions] from all over, and in ten months the project was completed" (Takeuchi 1971–1991, 30:161–162 [doc. 23020]).[3] According to the inscription, the project was initiated by a layman named Shirō. The daikanjin was the monk Sonkai of the local temple Zen'yōji, a branch of Nara's Saidaiji. Jissen of Saidaiji was *bugyō* (official in charge); the inscription also lists a layman surnamed Fujiwara, whose role is unclear. The actual work of clearing the river was supervised by I Yukitsune, probably a member of the I school of stone sculptors active throughout western Japan in the Kamakura period and often associated with Nara temples.

In the minds of kanjin solicitors, both temple building and public works projects had substantial religious value, and in this regard there was little distinction between them. Two documents regarding construction projects at Kumetaji illustrate this point. The first was a request issued in 1280 for the repair of temple buildings. The monks opened the request with a general appeal to the temple's "supporting families *(ujibito)*, the commoners (shomin) of the province and the people in cities and the countryside, far and near, of high and low estate, and of clerical or lay status." Having thus addressed the request to all possible givers, the monks went on to claim that the temple had been founded by Gyōki and honored with a visit from Emperor Shōmu. Donors were urged to give even a small amount, because "an insignificant act will produce a splendid result"—in other words, salvation (Takeuchi 1971–1991, 18:349–350 [doc. 13946]). The document then likened the founding of the temple to the rebuilding of Hsiang-shan temple in the ancient Chinese capital of Lo-yang and compared Gyōki with its restorer, declaring both to be manifestations of Monju.

The second document, issued in 1289, details Zenni's plans to finance the repair of the temple's irrigation pond through the sale of amulets. The construction of the pond was attributed to Gyōki, who had vowed that the temple would "protect the secular law and benefit all beings." The document explains that many miracles had occurred at the pond, including the appearance of kami and Buddhist guardian deities; dipping a hand or foot in its water would enable one to reach buddhahood. With the passage of time, however, the embankments of the pond had crumbled, so that "water from the pond seeps through large gaps in the retaining wall, rapidly inundating and destroying villagers' houses, gardens, and fields." Zenni then laments the temple's lack of social responsibility in failing to deal with the problem earlier (Takeuchi 1971–1991, 22:197–198 [doc. 16906]).

It is likely that the pond, which Zenni describes as "stretching more than fifty chō," was more than just a decorative feature at the temple. Rather, it was probably a reservoir that supplied irrigation water to surrounding villages. According to Miura Keiichi, the project was accomplished with the help of Andō Renshō, a powerful Hōjō retainer who had purchased the temple's *bettōshiki* (administrative position) in 1277 and had made a major contribution to the 1280 building project (1978:6–9). It is likely that Renshō was inspired by more than religious faith: Miura sees his involvement as part of an attempt by the Hōjō to assert their authority over local warriors and landholders. As Miura explains, the extension of existing irrigation structures led to the control of surrounding villages and their peasantry; this control may have been the intended result of the Kumetaji project.

If Miura is correct, then the small donors to the project—the villagers who purchased the stupa-amulets—were contributing to their own subjugation. They probably did not see it that way, however; nor, I expect, did Zenni launch his project for such Machiavellian reasons. Like his teacher Eizon, who came to the temple in 1282 to give alms to hinin, Zenni probably viewed public works projects as the acts of bodhisattvas, earning salvation for those who requested donations and those who gave them.

Restoring a Local Temple: Jōshō and Jōdoji

Kanjin hijiri and local communities sometimes cooperated to construct temples as well as to build bridges. For example, the Bingo temple Jōdoji was restored in 1306 through the initiative of lay community leaders and Jōshō, a charismatic disciple of Eizon (Takeuchi 1971–1991, 30:39–40, 41–47 [docs. 22742, 22747]; *Hiroshima ken no chimei* 1982:388–389).

Tradition credits the lay saint Prince Shōtoku (574–622) with the founding of the temple, located at Onomichi, a busy port along the Inland Sea. In the fourteenth century, the land surrounding Jōdoji and its companion temple Mandaradō was held as Ōta estate by the Shingon complex at Mt. Kōya. The temples may have served as the center where Kōya officials oversaw the shipping of shōen dues from the port. By the end of the thirteenth century, however, Jōdoji had fallen into disrepair. Two documents tell the story of the temple's restoration and the kanjin campaign that financed it. The first, a donation letter dated 1306, was signed by Enshin, a wealthy local merchant who had taken Buddhist orders and obtained the temple's bettōshiki (Takeuchi 1971–1991, 30:39–40 [doc. 22742]). In this document Enshin gave the temple's rebuilding effort the proceeds of Jōdoji's bettōshiki and that of Mandaradō, as well as some surrounding land—rewards he had obtained as *azukaridokoro* (custodial official) of Ōta manor.

Jōshō told his own story in a long aside in a deposition concerning Jōdoji holdings (Takeuchi 1971–1991, 30:41–47 [doc. 22747]). Jōshō's deposition was ratified by a number of other signatures: nine monks, twelve novices (shami), six saikai, and five kechienshu, including Enshin. The saikai probably assisted Jōshō in collecting donations, though the personal tone of his description suggests that he played an active part in the process; the kechienshu were doubtless the major donors to the project.

According to the document, several temple buildings had already been financed by a village elder who had taken the religious name Kōamida. Jōshō's efforts resulted in several more structures. The major task was the construction of the Kondō, the building that Enshin had mentioned.

Jōshō was a warrior from Kii province who served the bakufu deputy at Rokuhara in Kyōto. A carouser and a hunter, he developed the desire for enlightenment one evening in 1273 while drinking with friends. Thereafter he rejected his former life of violence and devoted himself to Kannon and Amida. Later he traveled to Nara where he sought out Eizon and asked the master's advice in solving a moral dilemma: he wanted to take religious orders, but he was an only son, and his father demanded that he marry and carry on the family line. To go against his father's wishes would be unfilial. Eizon replied that one could never truly repay the obligations to one's parents—except by embarking upon the path toward buddhahood. On his way home to Kii, the young warrior reached a river crossing. There he decided to take the tonsure, declaring, "If I'm still a layman the next time I cross this river, may I contract white and black leprosy before I die and in my next life fall into the limitless Avīci hell, from which there is no escape!" (Takeuchi 1971–1991, 30:43 [doc. 22747]). Armed with such resolve, he returned to Saidaiji, where he became Eizon's disciple. He studied at Saidaiji for more than twenty years, devoting himself to the clerical precepts, ascetic practice, the examination of both esoteric and exoteric teachings, and the worship of Kannon.

In 1298 Jōshō decided to carry Buddhist teachings to those in remote regions, and thus he headed west, intending to perform missionary work in Kyūshū. On the way he stopped at Onomichi, lodging for the summer in the Mandaradō. When he expressed his determination to press on to Kyūshū, the local elders protested, saying, "You don't have to go to Kyūshū to benefit living beings; anyplace will do," and invited him to stay. Then, it seems, the elders prevailed upon him to help restore their temple. "And so," Jōshō wrote, "I preached to believers in the ten directions and constructed a temple building three bays wide and four deep. Thus we encouraged the practice of Buddhism, repaid the four obligations, and disseminated virtue" (Takeuchi 1971–1991, 30:43–44 [doc. 22747]).[4] The project was an extensive one that took eight years to complete.

The honzon of the reconstructed temple was to be the bodhisattva Kannon. Jōshō planned a kanjin campaign to finance the carving of the image, declaring that the donors' small contributions—"a small cutting tool or a scrap of wood"—would bind them to Kannon and secure for them the bodhisattva's salvific compassion. Luck was with Jōshō, however: "Even before I began the meritorious act of making a new honzon, Prince Shōtoku's Eleven-faced Kannon was suddenly revealed to me—lifesize and golden in color" (Takeuchi 1971–1991, 30:44 [doc. 22747]). The meaning of this passage is not entirely clear—did Jōshō discover the image in a storeroom or at another temple? Was it donated by a wealthy patron? Did it appear to Jōshō in a dream so that he might have it copied? Whatever the case, Jōshō found it useful to emphasize the fortuitous way in which the image came to be designated as the temple's honzon. The image was installed on a stone platform that contained records of donations to the kanjin effort (Takeuchi 1971–1991, 30:44 [doc. 22747]).

Though Jōshō sought donations from a wide geographical

area, it was mainly local people who responded. They not only made donations, they also participated actively in the kanjin campaign:

> Village men and women all helped out as much as they could. Old and young, we all bustled off to the east and to the west. Some of us preached to loggers deep in the mountains, seeking good timber from remote valleys; others persuaded fishermen along the coast to haul heavy boulders to shore. Even when our begging bowls were empty, we did not know the meaning of fatigue, and even when our clothes were tattered, we did not lament the chill. We broke ground and leveled the earth, making a solid foundation for the temple. Working together, we set the supporting pillars. (Takeuchi 1971–1991, 30:44–45 [doc. 22747])

The physical participation of monks and lay believers in kanjin collections and construction work reinforced the solidarity of community and temple—even more so, perhaps, when human effort seemed enhanced by miracles, such as the discovery of the image of Kannon that gave the bodhisattva's special blessing to the Jōdoji project.

Something of the same excitement, personal involvement, and sense of community pervades the description of another medieval project, the construction of the abbey church of St.-Denis in France in 1140. Abbot Suger, who initiated and guided the construction efforts, discusses how he obtained crucial materials. His first problem was suitable stone, which luckily was discovered at a nearby quarry. Suger relates a miracle that occurred while the stone was being extracted. It seems that some of the regular laborers had run off because of a severe rainstorm. Seventeen people who were standing by—some disabled persons and some boys, according to Suger—hurried to the quarry and prayed to Saint Denis for assistance.

> Then . . . they dragged out what a hundred and forty or at least one hundred men had been accustomed to haul from the bottom of the chasm with difficulty—not alone by themselves, for that would have been impossible, but through the will of God and the assistance of the Saints whom they invoked; and they conveyed it to the site of the church on a cart. Thus it was made known throughout the neighborhood that this work pleased Almighty God exceedingly. . . .

The project then required appropriate timbers for the church's roof beams. Told that there were none in the forests nearby, Suger went in search of them himself, much as Chōgen or Jōshō might have done:

> . . . I began to think in bed that I myself should go through all the forests of these parts, look around everywhere and alleviate those delays and troubles if [beams] could be found here. . . . We . . . began, with the courage of our faith as it were, to search through the woods; and toward the first hour we found one timber adequate to the measure. Why say more? By the ninth hour or sooner we had, through the thickets, the depths of the forests and the dense, thorny tangles, marked down twelve timbers (for so many were necessary) to the astonishment of all." (Panofsky 1979:91–97)

When the church was dedicated, verses inscribed above doors and the altar expressed the hope that Suger and donors to the project might be welcomed into paradise. Similarly, when the construction of Jōdoji was completed in 1306, Jōshō thanked the community for its assistance and predicted: "Because of ties with the Buddha formed by the donation of a small cutting tool, patrons will gaze upon the thirty-two marks of the Buddha, and those who have helped with a scrap of lumber will [like Shakyamuni] attain enlightenment under the bodhi tree" (Takeuchi 1971–1991, 30:46 [doc. 22747]). In both cases, the clergymen who headed the reconstruction projects claimed that divine assistance was combined with human effort to complete the work. Neither by itself would have been entirely sufficient; if divine blessing was required, human effort was no less necessary, for it implicated the community in the project and thus guaranteed continued community support.

Jōdoji and the Visitor Deity

Like Jōshō and Chōgen, kanjin hijiri often came from outside the community that they served. Paradoxically, their position outside the local social structure conferred unusual power upon them— power that resided in the same charisma possessed by the deities of Japanese folk religion that we can call Visitors.

The folk cults of Visitor deities can be contrasted with

another type of cult, that of the *ujigami* (tutelary deity), which was based on lineage, excluded outsiders, and embraced particularistic functions related to community welfare. The cult of the Visitor, however, welcomed all believers and had aims—such as personal salvation through faith—that anyone might fulfill (Hori 1968:30–34; Davis 1977:31).[5] The Visitor might be superhuman or simply charismatic, but even very human Visitors were often considered the descendants of kami (for example, the emperor) or the incarnations of buddhas and bodhisattvas. The very outsiderhood of the Visitor meant that Visitor and ujigami cults had fundamentally different purposes. At the same time, as Winston B. Davis has pointed out, the Visitor or proponents of such a deity sought the cooperation of the local cult; Visitor and local cults were often amalgamated, and the former might even be absorbed by the latter (1977:32–33).

In the story of Jōshō and Jōdoji, there are three candidates for the Visitor: Kannon, Prince Shōtoku, and Jōshō himself. The first two had already "settled" at the temple and perhaps had been absorbed into the local religious system, which may have developed characteristics of an ujigami cult. At the very least, the temple claimed the loyalty of local people such as Kōamida. Chafing at their inability to restore the abandoned temple, the Onomichi faithful sought the help of someone with charismatic power. For his part, Jōshō could muster not only his own power as a holy man from a distant place, a disciple of the famous Eizon, and a man of distinguished bushi background, but also the power of Japan's greatest Buddhist layman and the compassionate bodhisattva Kannon. This latter power had resulted from a fortuitous, perhaps even a miraculous, discovery. Yet charismatic power could not accomplish the task alone: the local residents themselves mobilized resources and labor. Indeed, Jōdoji's welfare soon became the responsibility of the community: when all the temple buildings burned in 1325, they were restored over a period of some twenty years by a local couple, who initiated a kanjin campaign for the project (*Sōgon Jōdoji enyū jitsuroku,* quoted in *Hiroshima ken no chimei* 1982:388).

The construction of Jōdoji must be seen, however, against a background of struggle among representatives of the central proprietary class (including large temples and shrines), the bakufu, and local notables and holders. Ōta shō, the productive manor where the temple was located, had long been the object of dispute between its proprietor, Kongōbuji Konpondaitō at Mt. Kōya, and its jitō (*Hiroshima ken no chimei* 1982:334–335). The *jitōshiki* was initially held by the Tachibana family, shōen officials descended from the people who had originally reclaimed the land. In the Kamakura period, the Tachibana became retainers of the Bingo *shugo* (provincial military governor), and their rights were recognized as jitō rights—in other words, they were ratified by Kamakura. The original proprietor of the shōen, Go Shirakawa, donated his income rights to Kōya in 1187. In the following year, the temple dispatched the kanjin hijiri Hokkebō Kakua to Ōta estate as their on-site representative, or azukaridokoro. It may have been a quarrel between the azukaridokoro and the jitō that led to a lawsuit in 1195 accusing the latter of mistreating the shōen's peasants. Kamakura ordered them to desist and soon afterward withdrew their jitō rights. They were replaced by Miyoshi Yasunobu (1140–1221) of the Monchūjō, the bakufu's chief investigative agency. After the Jōkyū war of 1220–1221, Yasunobu's son settled on the estate. Thereafter the jitōshiki was divided between two Miyoshi scions, one who remained on site and another who turned over his duties to a surrogate. The surrogate gradually lost control to the azukaridokoro, who vied with the on-site jitō for the support of local holders and lesser shōen officials. As was the case on many other shōen, the jitō sometimes neglected to forward the proprietor's share of income. Thus, sometime in the late thirteenth century, Kōya appointed Enshin to the azukaridokoro post, in hopes that the powerful merchant would protect the temple's interests. The disputes between jitō and azukaridokoro continued, however; it was probably this tension that led local holders and shōen officials to accuse Enshin of living and dressing luxuriously, keeping a household of more than one hundred women and children, inviting female entertainers to his home day and night, and traveling from place to place in grand processions. The implication was that he had misappropriated shōen funds and overtaxed the peasants. Because of these charges, he lost the azukaridokoro post, but he retained the bettōshiki of Jōdoji and Mandaradō, which he had received as a reward for winning an earlier lawsuit.

   In 1302 a judgment from Kamakura divided jurisdiction over the Ōta estate holdings, giving part to the proprietor and part to the jitō in a standard compromise known as *shitaji chūbun* (Takeuchi 1971–1991, 28:17–18 [doc. 21111]). Judgments of this type were intended to resolve disputes over the control of territory and can be seen as a last-ditch method by absentee proprietors to fend off the depredations of on-site jitō (see Mass 1974b:157–183). The compromise underlined the need for Kōya to strengthen its grip on the territories left to it.

The shitaji chūbun document ratified Kōya's authority over Jōdoji and Mandaradō. As mentioned earlier, these temples were valuable to Kōya as a base from which to oversee shipments from Onomichi port. Enshin must have found them valuable for similar reasons: he had contracted to manage shipments bound for Tōdaiji and for Iwashimizu Hachiman shrine in Kyōto. Thus it was in the interests of both proprietor and temple bettō to restore the temple buildings and put them under firm control. The specter that lurked in the background was the powerful Miyoshi family, with its bakufu connections and its claim to jurisdiction over substantial shōen territory. On the surface it seems ironic, therefore, that the man chosen to supervise Jōdoji's reconstruction was a former bakufu retainer and the disciple of Eizon, whom the bakufu held in great respect.

Yet Jōshō may have been acting as a bakufu agent, as did other Ritsu monks of Eizon's Saidaiji line who were employed to advance bakufu interests, especially along the Inland seacoast. Amino Yoshihiko argues that this activity was connected with the efforts of the bakufu regents, the Hōjō, to establish control over Inland Sea shipping routes and ports (1974:297–302). Amino points out that Saidaiji monks conducted many of their projects in territories, especially port towns, under direct Hōjō control. In addition to Jōdoji, Amino cites the construction of the Saidaiji branch temple Myōōin at Ashida, a Bingo port that handled considerable domestic and foreign trade; the dredging of the Nariwa river mentioned earlier in this chapter; the kanjin activities of Kumetaji's bettō Gyōen, who collected donations for an anchorage at the mouth of the Kako river in Harima; and Ninshō's efforts to repair several anchorages in Settsu, including Chōgen's old project at Uozumi and the port of Watanabe, used in Chōgen's day as a way station for logs shipped from Suō to Tōdaiji. The Hōjō retainer Andō Renshō contributed heavily to these construction efforts, perhaps for reasons of his own, since he was engaged in commercial shipping (Amino 1974:294–295). Another prominent lay donor was Taira Shigemori,[6] probably a Hōjō retainer, who led seventy others in sponsoring an image of Jizō on a boulder in Sagishima harbor in Bingo. The sculptor was Nenshin, associated with Saidaiji-line temples. The story of the Ōwatashi bridge and the construction of Daijiji suggests that Hōjō efforts to use temples to control coastal territory were limited neither to the Inland Sea nor to Saidaiji Ritsu temples. The detailed examination of Jōdoji's history presented above, however, indicates that the picture is more complicated than Amino suggests. Jōdoji's reconstruction benefited Enshin and Kōya as much as it did the Hōjō. Moreover, the deposition of 1306 indicates that it was the Onomichi elders, including Kōamida, who initiated the project and solicited Jōshō's help. Yet Enshin was no local favorite; there seems to have been no obvious reason for local elders to want to help him out.

We cannot know for certain, but the temple's construction might have been an effort at making peace among four parties: the jitō, the proprietor, Enshin, and the local community. Each obtained something of value: the community got its temple, Enshin and Kōya were guaranteed a base for their Onomichi operations, and the jitō's Hōjō masters saw the temple come under control of a monk who had once been their retainer. The story of Jōdoji suggests a dynamic in which compromise and bargaining were important elements. That Saidaiji monks should have taken part in this effort should come as no surprise, considering their efforts in working for the public good and harmony in other situations.

Kanjin and Construction Work: Acts of Piety

Kanjin hijiri worked through the local leadership, but a successful campaign required them to attract donations from broad segments of the populace. The charismatic power attributed to the Visitor helps to explain how they did so, especially when they were not ordinary muen hijiri or saikaishū but distinguished men such as Jōshō and Giin, whose status and learning set them apart from most local people. Nor was this power simply a result of some mystical aura that adhered to outsiderhood: the Visitor was expected to furnish goods or services of practical benefit for the lay community. Instead of the bushels of rice supplied, in myth, by deities of the Visitor type, the kanjin hijiri provided fundraising skills, managerial ability, and technical expertise. The land reclamation skills of Giin and Jissen, for example, must have advanced the general economic growth and technological progress of their adopted communities, impressing not only leaders but ordinary folk as well.

Still, it is not clear why the local magnates who often encouraged such projects agreed to finance them through cumbersome kanjin campaigns. One answer is that local magnates enhanced their own power and prestige by mobilizing apparently willing assistance for their projects from the populace. Like Go Shirakawa, local leaders used kanjin for their own political ends.

Public works projects, moreover, had intrinsic religious meaning that justified the use of the kanjin method. As in medieval Europe (Brooke and Brooke 1984:24), such projects were regarded as acts of piety. Thus legends made no distinction between Gyōki's temples and his roads, and Giin proffered the Buddha's pity for all creatures as a reason for building the Ōwatashi bridge. Miura Keiichi has suggested that such work was considered to be a bosatsu gyō, the act of a bodhisattva and thus completely justifiable in religious terms (1978:5-6). The bodhisattva ideal of service to others permeated the practice of medieval Japanese Buddhism, with some very practical results for the social and economic welfare of the lay population.

In discussing their work, both Giin and Jōshō employed language that suggests that they saw very little difference between the work of construction and the work of evangelism. Arguing for the bridge, Giin wrote: "The Buddha said that those who have not crossed over [the river] will be enabled to cross it"; the passage can also be understood to mean "those who have not attained enlightenment will be enabled to attain it" (Takeuchi 1971-1991, 16:266 [doc. 12348]). When Jōshō related how fishermen were persuaded to "haul heavy boulders to shore" (Takeuchi 1971-1991, 30:45 [doc. 22747]), he used the terms *hiseki* (stubborn as a stone) and *tōgan* (to arrive at the shore of Buddhist salvation), imparting to the phrase a special Buddhist meaning: to pull stubborn unbelievers across the sea of *samsara* (the cycle of death and rebirth) to nirvana. The whole episode, in fact, is full of physical metaphors suggesting the equivalence of building temples and saving souls. The equation was the same in other cases, even when the construction project was a bridge rather than a temple.

Another religious value of kanjin efforts lay in the special regard for collective action found in contemporary Buddhist teachings. The common kanjin appeal—that no matter how small the donations, they would accumulate to produce great results— was more than an attempt to open the purses of people of limited means. Adapting the *yūzū nenbutsu* teachings of Ryōnin (1071– 1132), kanjin hijiri maintained that each good deed benefited not only the doer, but also all other participants, past, present, and future (Gorai 1975:40). Contributing to a kanjin effort could be seen as more meritorious than sponsoring an entire project on one's own. Like collective rituals such as the gyakushu of 1296 mentioned earlier in this chapter, kanjin efforts were often religious acts that reinforced community solidarity.

The kanjin hijiri's secret of success was the ability to address both economic and religious needs. Efforts that aimed simultaneously to save people's souls and to improve their welfare must have been more powerful in spreading Buddhism than those directed only toward the soul or toward the purse. Religious and secular projects, moreover, were not necessarily distinguished or viewed as contradictions. Both served the community in practical ways, and both could be justified in religious terms. If a bridge was the work of the Buddha, a temple served as a center of communal life and action, a repository of village records, and a storehouse of expertise. In summary, the construction projects of kanjin hijiri contributed to the popularization of Buddhism in three ways: they helped to endear the hijiri—and their religious teachings—to local notables who might influence others in the community; they associated Buddhism with practical good works that helped all people in their daily lives; and they enabled people to participate in such works, increasing their hopes of salvation, reinforcing their faith in the value of collective action, and strengthening the bonds of communitas.

—————————— Six ——————————

CONSTRUCTING THE BUDDHIST LAW

Kamakura Buddhism was a complex phenomenon, created not only by the founders of new sects, but also by monks of the ken-mitsu schools, vagabond hijiri, and lay believers. The interactions among these participants constructed new roads to paradise and new bridges between Buddhist institutions and the community at large. The needs of the lay community informed the way that the Buddhist message was promoted and received, often reshaping both message and community. This interactive process was enhanced by the search for religious validation on the part of such lay institutions as the throne, the village, and the lineage. It was furthered as well by the dual character of the monastic establishment as the source of religious truth and the salvation of all beings, on the one hand, and as an institution with powerful political and economic interests, on the other. The kanjin campaign, which both facilitated and depended on the interaction between monastic institution and lay believer, provides an ideal window through which to view this process.

This study of kanjin campaigns has suggested some interrelated propositions about medieval Japanese Buddhism that have both historical and historiographical implications. First, Japanese Buddhism was built on a physical framework of temples, pagodas, images, and sūtras. Neither clergy nor lay believers ignored this framework in favor of some disembodied notion of "doctrine"; for scholars to do so results in an unrealistic separation between formal teaching and actual practice that privileges the former and dismisses the latter as compromise or heresy.

Second, the construction of this framework required an interaction between monastic and lay communities that involved a search for power, a search often undertaken with radically different aims on the part of each party. Thus it is necessary to consider religious developments within their social and economic context. To do so is not to privilege religious ideas, on the one hand, or politics and economics, on the other, but simply to recognize their interrelatedness.

Third, both the construction of the framework and the search for power were best accomplished through enticing the voluntary cooperation of others. The importance of this principle to Buddhist institutions and to their lay supporters needs to be recognized, even though it was often violated in fact. Scholars who argue that coercion was the norm simply because it was so common are ignoring the frequent attempts to mask it.

Finally, the concept of voluntary participation, whether real or fictional, could be used to form organizations and to impel actions that lay outside or even opposed the social structure in which both temples and powerful lay patrons were embedded. Thus collectivities might be produced that transcended the divisions of medieval society, relying on the bonds of communitas rather than those of hierarchy and ascription. The many collectivities of this sort that arose in the Muromachi period lie outside the purview of this study, which I have limited to the early medieval age. Still, I will indulge in some speculation, while suggesting questions for further research.

Buddhism's physical framework was central to the program of preservation, restoration, and construction that underlay the revival of the kenmitsu schools. Using kanjin campaigns as a tool, solicitors offered lay believers a way to participate in this program. This activity was significant for the spread of Buddhist teachings not only for the obvious reason—that it enhanced the financial health of temples and thus enabled them to perform their religious duties—but also because, in the conceptual scheme of the time, building a temple was equated with constructing the Buddhist law. Thus, when kanjin solicitors earmarked donations to support a particular building or image, they were doing far more than creating a system of resource allocation.

Solicitors often appealed to the donor's senses, using highly pictorial detail to describe such things as the temple's past glory, its current dilapidated state, and the project under way. The Kasagidera kanjin appeals, for example, focused the potential donor's attention on the mountain where the temple was situated and on the temple's honzon, the image of Miroku:

On this mountain are the footprints of holy wizards; it is Jison's [Miroku's] sacred place. Although people may doubt what they hear about the mysterious founding of the temple and the splendor of the image, when they see, then they must believe. The image will remain unchanged throughout the appearance on earth of a thousand Buddhas [at the ends of successive kalpas]. How much more so will it remain constant until the day that Miroku descends to preach three times beneath the dragon flower tree! (Sōshō 1960:241)

The passage begins by establishing this particular mountain as a holy place and attributing its sanctity to the temple's central image. It goes on to invoke the power of the image to inspire faith in those who see it, then links the image with the supreme moment of Buddhism in the future, the coming of Miroku to evangelize all humankind. In short, physical phenomena define sanctity, arouse faith, and provide the occasion for the conferral of supreme rewards. Moreover, the claim that the image would endure for kalpa after kalpa attested to the durability of the Buddhist law itself.

At the most basic level, it might be argued that, in some cases, Buddhist truth could only be transmitted through physical means. Kūkai eloquently justified art as such a means in notes accompanying a list of artworks imported from China: "Truth is neither words nor color nor form. Although words may be used in transmitting truth, people can be made to *feel* truth only by means of forms and colors. Esoteric teachings hold that profound truths are difficult to express in written or spoken words. For those who find enlightenment on subtle points difficult, it is essential to resort to pictorial representations to inspire a sense of hidden meanings" (Sawa 1972:86).

If such claims could be made for paintings and sculpture, they could also apply to temple buildings themselves. Though strictly speaking attachment to grandeur and beauty were considered illusions that hampered one from attaining buddhahood, in fact grand and beautiful buildings might spark the desire for enlightenment and turn an individual toward salvation.

Kūkai's argument employed the concept of hōben, in which methods of teaching and propagation were fashioned to suit the audience. On a deeper level, it was also an expression of *hongaku*, the nondualistic thought that dominated Buddhist thinking from

Kūkai's time throughout the medieval age. As William R. LaFleur has pointed out, hongaku refused to subordinate means to ends and symbols to what they symbolize (1983:20–25). Dualism of the sort that might privilege mind over body or the "spiritual" over the physical was simply rejected.

Following the lead of Kūkai and most other significant Japanese Buddhist thinkers, the monks who built Tōdaiji and Jōdoji based their activities on this nondualistic philosophy. In the world that the monks imagined, temples were not only vehicles for spreading the Buddhist law, they became the Buddhist law itself; thus when a temple was preserved, restored, or constructed, the Buddhist law was as well. Temples—and bridges too, since there was no clear line between sacred and secular worlds—were part of the physical framework in which the Buddhist law was realized and would continue to be realized even in the darkest days of mappō. Their construction, moreover, was seen as an act of salvation for all who participated in it, whether solicitor, carpenter, or donor—making it necessary to invite broad participation in the form of donations to kanjin campaigns. Hongaku teachings allied Nara monks, vagabond hijiri, and lay believers, and made all three the instruments of religious change.

The urge to construct the Buddhist law through constructing its physical framework inspired the kanjin activities of such diverse figures as Jōkei, Chōgen, and Eizon, as well as the countless muen hijiri who plied city streets and the countryside in search of donations. Early Kamakura period thinkers such as Jōkei set the agenda for the revival of the Nara schools, constructing it on the twin axes of adherence to the precepts (for monks) and expedient means (for lay believers). Practical men such as Chōgen not only built the physical framework in which the Nara revival would be realized, but linked construction to religious action in the form of the nenbutsu. Once the philosophical and physical scaffolding of the Nara revival had been established, Ritsu monks such as Eizon and his followers could finish the structure with charity, public works, and rites for the dead—acts that redounded to the public benefit and thus involved Buddhist institutions deeply and inextricably in community life.

When Buddhism became part of the daily lives of the populace, it assumed an additional task, that of validating new social arrangements in a changing secular world. Just as in medieval

Europe, the expansion of wealth and power beyond the old elite classes led to new types of religious action. The European economy witnessed an increase in agricultural productivity, the penetration of money into rural life, and technological innovations that enhanced both trade and agriculture. Along with these changes in secular society came religious change: an explosion of church building, supported in part by alms campaigns, church involvement in secular public works projects such as the construction of roads and bridges, the emergence of hermit-preachers who dispensed charity along with the gospel, and the invention of new concepts (such as purgatory) to accommodate an expanding middle class.

In Japan, too, economic and religious change went hand in hand. The growth of the economy created a new class of people who threatened the power that temples held as shōen proprietors but whose prosperity and influence made them apt targets for proselytization. When small landholders reclaimed fields and kept the profits for themselves, bushi networks claimed power over land and cultivators, and artisans liberated themselves from single patrons and obtained the right to travel and trade freely, the stage was set for the development of a middle class that would demand religious validation of its institutional arrangements. Since power lay in continuity and connections, such people sought ties with the past and with their neighbors. These ties were found, at least in part, in rites performed by Buddhist monks and in organizations centered on local Buddhist temples. In addition, the greater part of this middle class was composed of warriors or warrior-farmers, whose need to take human life in violation of Buddhist precepts required the same expiation and toleration that Christianity extended to the medieval European moneylender. Thus changes in society provided a matrix in which Buddhism might also change and grow.

The principle of voluntary cooperation underlay temples' efforts to construct the Buddhist law and lay donors' efforts to validate their power and their institutions. In reality, many kanjin campaigns employed an element of coercion—not only in obvious forms such as tax levies or direct orders, but also in the form of pressure from superiors or neighbors. Yet much was made of the willing gift, and kanjin appeals generally enticed donations by promising rewards rather than by threatening punishments. Voluntary cooperation had obvious advantages for temples and for donors: it permitted kanjin solicitors to argue and donors to believe that their gifts would result in salvation. Monks who too obviously coerced donations could be accused of accumulating private wealth in violation of the precepts. Moreover, voluntary cooperation implied that donors recognized the authority of the elites (both national and local) who identified themselves with certain kanjin campaigns. For example, Go Shirakawa might have had Tōdaiji reconstructed through tax assessments alone, but instead he seized the opportunity to enhance his claims to authority over the entire nation while restoring a central imperial symbol. The importance of the principle of voluntary cooperation is underlined by the way in which that principle was violated. Even when participation was in fact forced (as with the assessment of tolls and taxes for temple support), it was masked as cooperation (by the use of the name kanjin for these levies). Although masks of this type rarely fooled anyone, that they were continually applied suggests the reluctance of power holders to apply overt methods of coercion. To do so would destroy the prospect of creating communal bonds between temple and donor that might endure to a later day.

A pivotal role in negotiating between temple and donor was assumed by the kanjin hijiri, whose ability to do so was enhanced by their muen status. Kanjin hijiri appeared in various guises, sometimes as shills, sometimes as builders, sometimes as undertakers and grave diggers. Perhaps it was their very ambiguity— their purity and piety often in doubt, their means venal and their ends sacred, their place unfixed in physical, social, and religious terms—that enabled them to perform a task that required the integration of different classes of people and radically different approaches to religious action.

Ambiguity had its drawbacks for the hijiri: it made them seem dangerous and encouraged people to view them with suspicion. Monks such as those from Chinkōji and Tōshōdaiji looked on kanjin hijiri as extortionists or charlatans. By the Muromachi period, hijiri were regarded with some disdain and were often categorized as hinin or beggars. Even worse, the sixteenth-century general Oda Nobunaga accused the hijiri of Mt. Kōya of spying for his enemies and put nearly 1400 of them to death (Gorai

1975:268). Rather than spies, beggars, or charlatans, however, most kanjin hijiri were probably simple folk like the villagers who gave them small donations and depended on them to dig wells or construct roads.

The power of the hijiri was derived from their ability to cross both literal and symbolic borders: to travel without constraint, to break monks' rules and claim the status of holy men, to work for temples while refusing to "belong" to them. Other borders might be crossed as well: there were hijiri who presented themselves (and were presented in literary sources) as shamans who crossed the boundary between the worlds of the living and the dead; this status gave them tremendous power in a society that feared death not only as an "undiscovered country," but as a constant source of danger for the living. Even their association with hinin and beggars gave them the "power of the weak"—the moral and ritual authority that, in Victor Turner's view, makes outsiders and marginals (Amino's muen individuals) the representatives of humanity as a whole and helps them to win power to which their position in the social structure does not entitle them (1974:234–235).

The muen status of kanjin hijiri put them in an ideal position to promote the concept of collective action. Although a single donation might be nothing but half a penny or a speck of dust, the accumulation of many contributions could work wonders: this was the central message of the kanjin hijiri. Thus kanjin campaigns, whether for temples, leprosariums, or bridges, had the potential to form collectivities. Some were no doubt ephemeral, limited to the specific project at hand, but others were marked by enduring ties; for instance, donors' adoption of the *amidabutsu* suffix may have signified long-term associations. But it was the kanjin rollbook, which recorded names of donors and their gifts, that most clearly established the existence of a community of donors. When the rollbook was stored inside a holy image, as it often was, it was further imbued with the sanctity of the buddha or bodhisattva that the image represented; I suspect, too, that it was meant to endure at least until the kalpa's end.

It probably took no great leap of imagination to apply the concept of the value of collective religious action to other types of action, including those of petition and protest. Local temples, in fact, sometimes served as centers for political action. For instance, in 1252, when local leaders and peasants on an Izumi province shōen demanded tax relief from the proprietor, their petition was entrusted to the village temple (Tanaka 1984:6). The temple became an ally of the local community in its attempt to gain relief —if not autonomy—from the proprietor in a time when local people were increasingly taking power and wealth into their own hands.

In his study of the medieval shōen system, Thomas Keirstead points out the importance of the concept of collectivity in peasant actions of resistance. Oaths signed by rebellious peasants were enacted at a ritual that claimed the solidarity of all participants, regardless of their usual antagonisms: "The ritual context that informed acts of resistance thus began by conceiving a collectivity, by posing against the divisions of everyday life a vision of communitas." This emphasis on solidarity, Keirstead argues, was part of a common language through which peasants and elites made themselves understood to one another. Peasants emphasized their solidarity not only for practical reasons but because "the claim of corporate identity [was] necessary to act in a world articulated through corporate bodies" (Keirstead 1992:82–87). Elites, religious institutions among them, commonly stressed the need for united action; as examples Keirstead cites rules and injunctions at Jingoji and Tōji.

The kanjin campaign may have been one medium through which the language and the model of collective action reached the peasant on the shōen. If so, it came imbued with religious meaning, including the promise of salvation for all participants and even for others that they designated. Tremendous power inhered in a concept of collective action whose results extended beyond the present world but had demonstrable this-worldly implications: in an age when farmers as well as bushi were beginning to claim the fruits of increased agricultural productivity, kanjin provided a model that could help them transform their new economic position into political power.

Protest, resistance, and enhancing the political power of non-elites were hardly on the agenda of the temples that initiated kanjin campaigns. The irony is that Buddhist temples, especially the great ones, were an arm of the central elite. Even when that elite largely crumbled in the Muromachi period, temples were surprisingly resilient, maintaining lands and developing new sources of wealth and control when the lay aristocracy was in almost total eclipse. But as the imperial court in the days of Gyōki knew very well, Buddhism had the potential to subvert the existing order as well as to support it. Language and models furnished by the most enduring representatives of the old order could be turned against that order and could assist in its destruction. The kanjin model may have borne additional fruit in the Muromachi period, when people banded together to advance their own interests in ways that they had not done before. Peasants formed village communities that wrested control of crucial functions, such as irrigation and taxation, from shōen proprietors (Nagahara 1977:107–123). Lower-level bushi and then peasants created *ikki*, leagues based on principles of egalitarianism and voluntary participation, that frequently turned to violent means to secure their demands (Davis 1974:221–247). Collective action often had religious inspiration: the famous Ikkō Ikki that dominated Kaga province in the late Muromachi period was organized by adherents of the Jōdo Shinshū sect. It may be that such movements were modeled ultimately on examples of collective action promoted by kanjin hijiri in the Kamakura age—not only the campaigns themselves, but also the lay societies, kechienshu or *kō*, that people formed for religious purposes. (It is probably no accident that kō were particularly important among lay followers of Jōdo Shinshū, providing "the economic as well as the social foundation" for the sect [Solomon 1972:276].) In short, even as temples used means of persuasion (kanjin) to reinforce their ancient authority, ideas spread by kanjin solicitors may have contributed to the chaos and social mobility that characterized the late Muromachi age.

The potential of muen hijiri to undermine systems of authority may help to explain the fate of many of them at the hands of Oda Nobunaga. Emiko Ohnuki-Tierney proposes that structural marginality provides certain figures "with the basis for becoming mediators when cross-categorical traffic is in need, and for becoming scapegoats when the structure calls for the reinforcement of boundary markers" (1987:218). Her remarks concern monkeys and special status people (including but not limited to hinin), but perhaps they can be applied to hijiri as well, especially in the Muromachi period, when hijiri were often hard to distinguish from beggars and outcasts. Nobunaga's program was to create a political realm *(tenka)* that embraced all structures of authority, including that of Buddhism; his violent suppression of certain Buddhist institutions such as the Ikkō Ikki and the monasteries on Mt. Hiei has been explained as a means toward that end (see McMullin 1984). The triumph of Nobunaga and his successors Toyotomi Hideyoshi and Tokugawa Ieyasu can be seen in part as the triumph of one type of social structure over another, as John W. Hall has pointed out (1981:7–21). The victorious structure, which Hall calls feudal, was based on hierarchical principles and the concentration of power at the top. Warlords known as *daimyō* "sought to become absolute masters of land and people within their territories, aiming to reduce all samurai to vassalage and all peasants into dues-paying workers of the land." The opposing type of organization was the ikki. Hall maintains that ikki were ephemeral structures that eventually dissolved or were transformed into daimyō domains. Hall notes, however, the resiliency of those ikki that had a religious basis. But even they succumbed to the daimyō organizations "that had the capability of further expansion and ultimately the creation of a national hegemony" (1981:10).

The re-creation of order in the realm after more than a century of civil war required that boundaries be drawn, or at least the three unifiers seem to have thought so. Vagabond hijiri were a threat to these boundaries, since traversing them easily might be seen as a challenge to their validity. I suspect that Nobunaga was well aware of this when he had so many Kōya hijiri executed as spies. Even the slaughter of 1400 did not utterly destroy hijiri, although their influence and the independence of the religious universe in which they operated were drastically reduced. But can Nobunaga's action be explained simply as retribution for spying? Or did Nobunaga see some fundamental connections between the hijiri and dangerous collectivities such as the ikki?

All that is in the realm of speculation, but we can be more certain of the role that kanjin played in the arts of the Muromachi period. Ever in search of more effective methods to increase donations, temples expanded their use of entertainment for kanjin purposes, charging admission to theatrical performances such as *sarugaku, dengaku, nō* dancing, *sumō* wrestling, and recitals of the war chronicle *Heike monogatari;* and kanjin hijiri regularly trotted out picture scrolls in public places, using them to explain why one should donate to their temple (Sasaki 1987:81; Ruch 1977:299).

By this time kanjin had become a show for which people bought tickets, instead of a religious campaign to which they gave alms. I suspect, however, that hijiri had always been entertainers of a sort and that part of the reason that people gave to kanjin campaigns was because hijiri amused them. Religion and theater were, after all, not completely different things. Perhaps it is not inappropriate that the most common use of the term kanjin today is in the title of a popular *kabuki* play, *Kanjinchō,* which portrays warriors in disguise as kanjin hijiri.

In the Kamakura period, however, kanjin had a much broader role than that of entertainment. People enjoyed kanjin hijiri but also took them quite seriously, perhaps because their promises of salvation were backed by visible service in the daily world. Kanjin campaigns, moreover, gave life to abstract teachings by linking them with things that people could touch and see: sacred mountains, images, temples, and pagodas. The participation of hijiri and lay believers in preserving or making these things enabled them to construct vital new forms of popular religion on a concrete framework of image and holy place.

Notes

Chapter One

1. The term *kenmitsu* means, literally, exoteric *(kengyō)* and esoteric *(mikkyō)*. "Esoteric" is generally applied to the Shingon school, in which the most basic teachings were secret and were transmitted orally to a chosen few. "Exoteric" is applied to the Nara schools, which had originally relied on written tradition theoretically available to all; by the late Heian period, however, the Nara schools contained a significant esoteric component. The Tendai school combined both types of teachings, although esotericism was the more significant of the two in the period studied here.

2. Central to the reevaluation of Kamakura Buddhism is the analysis by Kuroda Toshio (1975, 1980) of the institutional power and internal structure of the kenmitsu schools, the examination by a team led by Gorai Shigeru (1964) of artifacts from the Nara temple Gangōji that prove an active role for kenmitsu temples in the spread of popular Buddhism, and the work of Amino Yoshihiko (1978b) on people and places—including temples and vagabond ascetics—outside the social mainstream based on landholding and agriculture. In-depth studies such as Nagamura Makoto's analysis of Tōdaiji (1980, 1981, 1989), Amino's work on Tōji (1978a), Hosokawa Ryōichi's examination of the Ritsu school (1987), and Gorai's study of ascetic evangelists at Mt. Kōya, a bastion of the Buddhist establishment (1975), have given us new perspectives on the activities of kenmitsu institutions in the Kamakura age. Important contributions have also been made by English-language works such as James H. Foard's study of Ippen (1977) and his redefinition of Kamakura Buddhism (1980); Robert E. Morrell's examination of religious pluralism with emphasis on the kenmitsu schools (1985, 1987); and James C. Dobbins' studies of Shinran, Rennyo, and the institutional development of the Jōdo Shinshū sect (1986, 1989).

3. A recent article by Neil McMullin (1989) and a subsequent exchange between McMullin (1992) and Jamie Hubbard (1992) in the *Japanese Journal of Religious Studies* make some of these points and identify some biases that I have tried to avoid in this book: privileging doctrine over practice (in McMullin's terms, over institutions and rituals)—or vice versa—and assuming that monks were corrupt because they had material interests.

4. The time from the death of the Buddha to the nadir of the Buddhist law is divided into three stages. In the first of these, the period of the true law, Buddhism can be taught and practiced, and enlightenment can be attained. In the second stage, that of the imitation law, only teaching and practice are possible; and in mappō only the teaching remains. These stages were assigned different lengths of time depending on the interpreter, but by the Heian period it was generally thought that the first two were to last for one thousand years each. Since the year of the Buddha's death had been mistakenly set as 949 B.C., the onset of mappō was calculated at A.D. 1052. See Marra 1991:71–75.

Chapter Two

1. The original text from which Kitagawa quotes can be found in Kuroita 1943:207–255.

2. As historical sources, *engi* are not entirely reliable, and some authorities have called this one into question. Since kanjin campaigns were not unusual for this period, however, I see no reason to doubt that one was conducted. The kanjin appeal recorded in the engi is a standard one and cash donations, while unusual, are not unprecedented.

Chapter Three

1. For interesting treatments of the sacralization of the mountains, see Grapard 1982, 1986, and 1989.

2. The diamond world represents wisdom, whereas the womb-store world represents the multiplicity of phenomena. Together the two worlds make up the universe in the esoteric Buddhist scheme.

3. The term *nenbutsu* has come to refer only to the invocation of Amida's name, but in the Heian and Kamakura periods, it included a number of practices, including the invocation of the names of Shakyamuni and Miroku and the contemplation of any buddha. The term could possibly refer to the ceremony of 1183 as well as the one of 1182.

4. Unless stated otherwise, Jōkei's biography is taken from Kamata and Tanaka 1971:461–469. A biographical sketch in English is provided by Morrell 1983 and Morrell 1987. For information on Jōkei's devotion to Kasuga shrine and the Kasuga Daimyōjin, see Tyler 1990 and Tyler 1992.

5. For a collection of essays on the Lotus sūtra in Japanese history, see Tanabe and Tanabe 1989. For a tenth-century collection of tales about the sūtra, see Inoue and Ōsone 1974:44–219, and Dykstra 1983.

6. *Kasagidera engi*, a late and therefore somewhat unreliable source, lists two holdings: ten chō of paddy and dry fields (donated in 1182 to

support perpetual readings of the Lotus sūtra) and Hachijō In's gift of 1196, jitō rights in Sohara *mikuriya*, shrine tribute lands in Ise province (1913:90–91). Since the Sohara holding is not mentioned in contemporary documents, I suspect that the engi compiler may have confused it with Sugimoto; the 1182 gift may be that of Go Shirakawa, although lacunae in the engi make it impossible to tell.

7. Miroku beliefs have their foundation in texts known collectively as the Three-Part Miroku sūtra (Takakusu and Watanabe 1924–1932, 14:421–435 [nos. 453–457]). The worship of Miroku in Japan has been documented by a number of Japanese scholars (e.g., Hayami 1971). For an English-language treatment, see Goodwin 1977. An examination of East and Southeast Asian beliefs and practices related to Miroku can be found in Sponberg and Hardacre 1988.

8. The quotations are taken from the translation in Morrell 1983:20–38. For the original, see Kamata and Tanaka 1971:31–42, 312–316.

Chapter Four

1. The date of the incident according to the current Western calendar would be January 1181, since a year in the old Japanese calendar system began about a month later than in the Western calendar. Japanese and Western years are treated here as if they corresponded exactly.

2. An English-language account of Tōdaiji's reconstruction and Chōgen's role in it can be found in Coaldrake 1986:42–44.

3. Biographical information on Go Shirakawa has been taken from the following sources: Gomi 1984:433–437; Hurst 1976:178–213 and 1982:7–10; McCullough 1988:2–6 and passim; and Takeuchi 1978:268–288.

4. Both Horiike (1976:4) and Asai and Asai (1986:14) state that temple lands were restored on 1181/3/1, without citing a source for this information. The fact that the last conversation between Go Shirakawa's representative and Kujō Kanezane reported in *Gyokuyō* that made an issue of the problem was dated 1181/intercalary 2/20 suggests that the lands were indeed restored soon after that date.

5. Translations of the imperial order and Chōgen's appeal into modern Japanese can be found in Hashimoto and Horiike 1940:118–120. For phrases that quote Shōmu's edict of 749 in the passages that I quote, I have generally used the translation in Tsunoda, de Bary, and Keene 1958, 1:104–105.

6. Large Buddhist images are often described as jōroku in height, referring to the mythical height of the historical Buddha. Although the measurement jōroku (1.6 *jō*) is almost equivalent to sixteen feet, it cannot

be taken literally in this case: the Daibutsu was actually more than fifty-three feet tall.

7. Two of the six *haramitsu,* the practices through which the bodhisattva attains nirvana.

8. This differs from the version in Tsunoda, de Bary, and Keene 1958, which reads "should pay homage daily to the image of Roshana, so that with constant devotion we can construct the image ourselves" (1:104–105).

9. For an overview of Chōgen's building projects, see Tanaka 1976.

10. Biographical information on Chōgen has been taken from the following sources: Amino 1975:364–368; Fukuda 1967; Gomi 1984:402–405; Gorai 1975; Kobayashi 1971; and Nakanodō 1975. For a collection of source materials concerning Chōgen, see Kobayashi 1965.

11. The term "Visitor" is my own; Yamaguchi uses the term "stranger." Other examinations of the Visitor (using other terminology) can be found in Hori 1968:30–34 and Davis 1977:28–31.

12. Details of this account are taken from Kobayashi 1971:85–104. I am also indebted to Arnesen (1982:100–105) for material about Tōdaiji and Suō province.

13. I am indebted to Kobayashi Takeshi (1971:101–300) for much of this information about the bessho. In addition, I have relied on Fukuda 1967; Horiike 1976:11–18; Nagamura 1980:50–51; and Tanaka 1976: 32–43.

14. Kobayashi Takeshi argues that since the temple was moved from Awa in Shikoku by a follower of the defeated Taira, the move probably took place no earlier than 1185, after the Minamoto victory at Dannoura; an inscription on an armrest reads "donated to the Tōdaiji nenbutsu center, 1187/9/2," and Kobayashi maintains that there was a connection between this center and Chōgen's base at Tōdaiji, Jōdodō (1971: 109–111). If they were the same, then the founding of Jōdodō can be set between 1185 and 1187.

15. For an English-language discussion of the carving of this image, see Kanda 1985:72–78.

Chapter Five

1. Biographical details on Eizon are taken from Kamata and Tanaka 1971:488–492; Yoshida 1972:205–209; and Wajima 1959:1–99.

2. For a discussion of a similar phenomenon in contemporary China, see Watson 1988.

3. Illegible characters in the inscription have necessitated omissions in the translation.

4. The four obligations are variously defined: to parents, teachers,

ruler, the Buddha, the Buddhist law, the Buddhist clergy, all living beings, and so forth.

5. Hori uses the term *hitogami* for the Visitor; Davis uses the term "adventitious deity" (*marōdogami*).

6. This is not the famous son of Taira Kiyomori, who appears as a prominent character in *The Tale of the Heike*.

Glossary

This glossary includes specialized terms that are used fairly frequently throughout the book. It is not intended as a complete listing; terms that are discussed briefly are generally defined only when they first occur in the text. Terms in common use in English-language textbooks on Japanese history are omitted.

Measures of capacity, length, and area were not standardized in medieval times. The equivalents given here are approximations.

azukaridokoro 預所 A shōen official, often the representative of the absentee proprietor.

bessho 別所 A subsidiary of a major temple, sometimes located in the mountains. Bessho were often gathering places for kanjin hijiri.

bettō 別当 An administrative official, often appointed by the court or bakufu to supervise an institution, such as a temple, that was not strictly speaking a government body.

bushi 武士 The warrior class.

chishiki 知識 Sanskrit: *mitra*. In kanjin documents, lay believers who support Buddhist temples. The characters suggest the wisdom of the Buddhist faithful.

chō 町 A unit of area, approximately 2.94 acres.

Daibutsu 大仏 The Great Buddha, an image of Roshana first constructed at Tōdaiji in the eighth century.

daikanjinshiki 大勧進職 A position at a temple sanctioned by the government (court or bakufu). The occupant of the position was charged with collecting donations for the temple and was often given broad responsibilities pertaining to construction and financial management.

engi 縁起 A collection of temple or shrine documents, legends, and inventories; often a running compilation to which monks made additions as they saw fit.

hijiri 聖 A term usually applied to an unorthodox religious figure who practiced ascetic regimens outside the auspices of monastic institutions. The term is a loose one. It can also designate a member of the regular clergy who had special charisma or was especially devoted to ascetic practice.

hinin 非人 Literally, "nonperson." The term was applied loosely to people cast out from society because of an occupation or condition considered ritually polluting or disgraceful.

hiseki 匪石 Stubborn and unmoving, like a stone.

hōben 方便 Sanskrit: *upāya*. The Buddhist doctrine of expedient means, which holds that evangelistic methods may be tailored to the believer and that any method is acceptable if it directs a person on the path toward salvation.

hongaku 本覚 The principle of original enlightenment. According to Tendai and Shingon Buddhist teachings, the seeds of enlightenment exist within each mind, and thus it is possible for one to be enlightened within the phenomenal world. According to LaFleur, hongaku rejected the dualism of body and mind, or of physical and nonphysical entities (1983:21).

honzon 本尊 The sculpture or painting considered to be the main focus of worship at a temple.

In-no-chō 院庁 The office of the retired emperor. Through this quasi-governmental apparatus, retired emperors in the late Heian and Kamakura periods exercised control over the distribution of land rights.

jitō 地頭 A steward on a shōen. In the Kamakura period, jitō were military men appointed by and responsible to the bakufu.

kanjin 勧進 A method of collecting donations for temples and shrines through public subscription campaigns. The term can also mean "evangelism."

kanmon 貫文, *kan* 貫 (1) A unit of coinage. In 1150 a piece of residential land of unspecified area in Yamato province was sold for twenty-seven kanmon (Mori 1973:27). (2) Kan also designates a unit of weight approximately equal to 3.75 kilograms.

kechienshu 結縁衆 A group of lay believers formed to fulfill a particular religious purpose, such as the dedication of a sūtra or the repair of a temple.

kenmitsu 顕密 Exoteric and esoteric. The term was applied to the established schools of Buddhism in the Heian and Kamakura periods. The kenmitsu schools included the traditional six schools of Nara, established prior to the Heian period, and the Heian schools of Tendai and Shingon.

koku 石 A unit of capacity equal to approximately 180 liters.

Kurōdodokoro 蔵人所 The Imperial Secretariat, which served as a private office for regnant or retired emperors.

mappō 末法 Sanskrit: *saddharma-vipralopa*. According to scripture, the fortunes of the Buddhist law begin to decline some five hundred years after the death of a buddha. Mappō is the final stage in this decline.

During this period it is thought to be difficult for people to attain salvation or enlightenment without either extraordinary effort (according to some analyses) or the grace of a buddha (according to others). Calculations accepted in medieval Japan set the beginning of mappō at A.D. 1052.

mon 文 A unit of coinage, .001 kanmon.

monme 匁 A unit of weight, .001 kan (definition 2).

muen 無縁 Literally, "unattached." The term has a wide range of connotations: it can indicate one who eschews social and political connections to seek out Buddhist enlightenment, one who has no official position and therefore has marginal status in society, or one who has died without descendants to maintain his or her ancestral tablets.

mujō 無常 Sanskrit: *anitya*. Impermanence, the Buddhist concept that every phenomenon is constantly changing.

munebechi sen 棟別銭 A tax levied on households for the support of temple and shrine construction projects.

nenbutsu 念仏 Sanskrit: *buddha-manasikāra*. The contemplation of a buddha. In medieval Japan, the term was often used to refer specifically to the recitation of a buddha's name.

Ritsu 律 Sanskrit: *Vinaya*. A school of Buddhist thought and practice that emphasizes the precepts that govern the Buddhist clergy. Also, monks who are devoted to the precepts.

ryō 両 A unit of weight, .01 kan (definition 2).

setsuwa 説話 Anecdotal literature, often with a basis in folklore and popular tales. Setsuwa usually have a didactic purpose and can be used to transmit Buddhist teachings on a popular level.

shiki 職 An official post with specific rights and obligations; also, the officially recognized right to income, usually from land.

shō 升 A unit of capacity, .01 koku. One shō of rice was considered enought to feed one person for a day.

shōen 荘園, 庄園 An estate or manor; a private holding recognized by the government. Shōen were not held outright by any single party; instead, several parties might hold rights to the income from the land.

shomin 庶民 Ordinary people; those without official positions in government or on a shōen.

shōnin 聖人, 上人 A title of honor given to a Buddhist practitioner considered to be especially virtuous and holy. In the first pair of characters for this term, the initial character means hijiri.

tan 段 A unit of area, .1 chō.

tōgan 到岸 To reach the "other shore" of Buddhist salvation.

yūzū nenbutsu 融通念仏 The belief that calling the name of Amida benefits not only oneself but others as well.

Select Bibliography

Amino Yoshihiko. 1972. "Chūsei ni okeru tennō shihaiken no hito kōsatsu: kugonin sakushu o chūshin toshite." *Shigaku zasshi* 81, 8.
———. 1974. *Mōko shūrai. Nihon no rekishi* 10. Tokyo: Shōgakukan.
———. 1975. "Chūsei shoki ni okeru imonoshi no sonzai keitai—Heian matsu, Kamakura zenki no tōro kugonin o chūshin ni." *Nagoya Daigaku Nihonshi ronshū* 1, ed. Nagoya Daigaku Bungakubu Kokushigaku Kenkyūshitsu.
———. 1978a. *Chūsei Tōji to Tōji ryō shōen.* Tokyo: Tōkyō Daigaku Shuppankai.
———. 1978b. *Muen, kugai, raku: Nihon chūsei no jiyū to heiwa.* Tokyo: Heibonsha.
Aoki Kazuo, Inaoka Kōji, Sasayama Haruo, and Shirafuji Noriyuki, eds. 1989–1990. *Shoku nihongi.* 2 vols. *Shin Nihon koten bungaku taikei.* Tokyo: Iwanami Shoten.
Arnesen, Peter J. 1982. "Suō Province in the Age of Kamakura." In *Court and Bakufu in Japan: Essays in Kamakura History,* ed. Jeffrey P. Mass. New Haven: Yale University Press.
Asai Kazuharu and Asai Kyōko. 1986. *Tōdaiji II (chūsei ikō). Nihon no koji bijutsu* 7. Osaka and Tokyo: Hoikusha.
Bloch, Marc. 1961. *Feudal Society.* Trans. L. A. Manyon. Chicago: University of Chicago Press.
Brooke, Christopher. 1987. *Europe in the Central Middle Ages, 962–1154.* 2d edition. London: Longman.
Brooke, Rosalind, and Christopher Brooke. 1984. *Popular Religion in the Middle Ages: Western Europe, 1000–1300.* London: Thames & Hudson.
Brown, Delmer M., and Ishida Ichirō. 1979. *The Future and the Past: A Translation and Study of the Gukanshō, an Interpretative History of Japan Written in 1219.* Berkeley: University of California Press.
Chōgen. 1934. *Namuamidabutsu sazenshū. Bukkyō geijutsu* 30.
Coaldrake, William H. 1986. "Architecture at Tōdai-ji." In *The Great Eastern Temple: Treasures of Japanese Buddhist Art from Tōdai-ji,* ed. Mino Yutaka. Chicago: Art Institute of Chicago in association with Indiana University Press.
Collcutt, Martin. 1981. *Five Mountains: The Rinzai Zen Monastic Institution*

in Medieval Japan. Cambridge, Mass.: Council on East Asian Studies, Harvard University Press.

Davis, David L. 1974. *"Ikki* in Late Medieval Japan." In *Medieval Japan: Essays in Institutional History,* ed. John W. Hall and Jeffrey P. Mass. New Haven: Yale University Press.

Davis, Winston B. 1977. *Toward Modernity: A Developmental Typology of Popular Religious Affiliations in Japan.* East Asia Papers Series. Ithaca: Cornell University Press.

Dobbins, James C. 1986. "From Inspiration to Institution: The Rise of Sectarian Identity in Jōdo Shinshū." *Monumenta Nipponica* 41:3.

————. 1989. *Jōdo Shinshū: Shin Buddhism in Medieval Japan.* Bloomington: Indiana University Press.

Dykstra, Yoshiko K. 1983. *Miraculous Tales of the Lotus Sutra from Ancient Japan: The Dainihonkoku Hokekyōkenki of Priest Chingen.* Hirakata, Osaka prefecture: Intercultural Research Institute, Kansai University of Foreign Studies.

Foard, James H. 1977. *Ippen Shōnin and Popular Buddhism in Kamakura Japan.* Ph.D. dissertation, Stanford University.

————. 1980. "In Search of a Lost Reformation: A Reconsideration of Kamakura Buddhism." *Japanese Journal of Religious Studies* 7:4.

Fujiwara Munetada. 1915–1916. *Chūyūki.* 7 vols. *Shiryō tsūran* 8–14, ed. Sasagawa Taneo. Tokyo: Nihon Shiseki Hozonkai.

Fukuda Harutsugu. 1967. "Tōdaiji bessho no hito kōsatsu." *Nanto bukkyō* 23.

Genkō shakusho. 1913. *Dainihon bukkyō zensho* 101. Tokyo: Bussho Kankōkai.

Gomi Fumihiko. 1984. *Inseiki shakai no kenkyū.* Tokyo: Yamakawa Shuppansha.

Goodwin, Janet R. 1977. "The Worship of Miroku in Japan." Ph.D. dissertation, University of California, Berkeley.

————. 1987. "Alms for Kasagi Temple." *Journal of Asian Studies* 46, 4.

————. 1989. "Building Bridges and Saving Souls: The Fruits of Evangelism in Medieval Japan." *Monumenta Nipponica* 44, 2.

————. 1989. "Shooing the Dead to Paradise." *Japanese Journal of Religious Studies* 16, 1.

————. 1990. "The Buddhist Monarch: Go-Shirakawa and the Rebuilding of Tōdai-ji." *Japanese Journal of Religious Studies* 17, 2–3.

Gorai Shigeru. 1964. *(Gangōji Gokurakubō) Chūsei shomin shinkō no kenkyū.* Kyoto: Hōzōkan.

————. 1975. *Kōya hijiri.* Tokyo: Kadokawa Shoten.

Graham, Rose. 1945–1947. "An Appeal about 1175 for the Building Fund of St. Paul's Cathedral Church." *Journal of the British Archaeological Association.* 3d series, vol. 10.

Grapard, Allan G. 1982. "Flying Mountains and Walkers of Emptiness: Toward a Definition of Sacred Space in Japanese Religions." *History of Religions* 20, 3.

————. 1986. "Lotus in the Mountain, Mountain in the Lotus: *Rokugō Kaizan Nimmon Daibosatsu Hongi.*" *Monumenta Nipponica* 41, 1.

————. 1989. "The Textualized Mountain—Enmountained Text: The *Lotus Sutra* in Kunisaki." In *The Lotus Sutra in Japanese Culture,* ed. George J. Tanabe, Jr., and Willa Jane Tanabe. Honolulu: University of Hawaii Press.

————. 1992. *The Protocol of the Gods: A Study of the Kasuga Cult in Japanese History.* Berkeley: University of California Press.

Hall, John W. 1981. "Japan's Sixteenth-Century Revolution." In *Warlords, Artists, and Commoners: Japan in the Sixteenth Century,* ed. George Elison and Bardwell L. Smith. Honolulu: University of Hawaii Press.

Harrington, Lorraine F. 1982. "Social Control and the Significance of *Akutō.*" In *Court and Bakufu in Japan: Essays in Kamakura History,* ed. Jeffrey P. Mass. New Haven: Yale University Press.

Hashimoto Shōjun and Horiike Shunpō. 1940. *Tōdaijishi.* Nara: Kegonshū, Tōdaiji.

Hayakawa Junzaburō, ed. 1923. *Azuma kagami.* 3 vols. Tokyo: Kokusho Kankōkai.

Hayami Tasuku. 1971. *Miroku shinkō—mō hitotsu no jōdo shinkō.* Tokyo: Hyōronsha.

Hiroshima ken no chimei. 1982. *Nihon rekishi chimei taikei* 35. Tokyo: Heibonsha.

Hirota, Dennis, trans. 1986. *No Abode: The Record of Ippen.* Kyoto: Ryukoku University.

Hori Ichirō. 1968. *Folk Religion in Japan: Continuity and Change.* Chicago: University of Chicago Press.

Horiike Shunpō. 1976. "Daioshō Chōgen shōnin no sazen." *Bukkyō geijutsu* 105.

Hosokawa Ryōichi. 1987. *Chūsei no risshū jiin to minshū.* Tokyo: Yoshikawa Kōbunkan.

Hubbard, Jamie. 1992. "Premodern, Modern, and Postmodern: Doctrine and the Study of Japanese Religion." *Japanese Journal of Religious Studies* 19, 1.

Hurst, G. Cameron, III. 1976. *Insei: Abdicated Sovereigns in the Politics of Late Heian Japan, 1086-1185.* New York: Columbia University Press.

————. 1982. "The *Kōbu* Polity: Court-Bakufu Relations in Kamakura Japan." In *Court and Bakufu in Japan: Essays in Kamakura History,* ed. Jeffrey P. Mass. New Haven: Yale University Press.

Inagaki Yasuhiko. 1975. "Chūsei no nōgyō keiei to shūshu keitai." In *Iwanami kōza Nihon rekishi* 6: *Chūsei* 2. Tokyo: Iwanami Shoten.

Inoue Mitsusada. 1956. *Nihon jōdokyō seiritsushi no kenkyū*. Tokyo: Yamakawa Shuppansha.

Inoue Mitsusada and Ōsone Shōsuke. 1974. *Ōjōden, Hokkegenki. Nihon shisō taikei* 7. Tokyo: Iwanami Shoten.

Ishida Mosaku. 1964. *Japanese Buddhist Prints*. English adaptation by Charles S. Terry. Tokyo: Kodansha International.

Ishida Yoshihito. 1975. "Tohi minshū no seikatsu to shūkyō." In *Iwanami kōza Nihon rekishi* 6: *Chūsei* 2. Tokyo: Iwanami Shoten.

Itō Kazuhiko. 1980. "Jōkei no kenkyū—Kasagi inton ni tsuite." In *Shōensei shakai to mibun kōzō*, ed. Takeuchi Rizō. Tokyo: Azekura Shobō.

Jien. 1969. *Gukanshō zenchūkai*. Ed. Nakajima Etsuji. Tokyo: Yūseidō Shuppan.

Kagawa ken no chimei. 1989. *Nihon rekishi chimei taikei* 38. Tokyo: Heibonsha.

Kakimura Shigematsu, ed. 1968. *Honchō monzui chūshaku*. 2 vols., orig. pub. 1922. Tokyo: Fuzanbō.

Kamata Shigeo and Tanaka Hisao. 1971. *Kamakura kyū bukkyō. Nihon shisō taikei* 15. Tokyo: Iwanami Shoten.

Kamens, Edward. 1988. *The Three Jewels: A Study and Translation of Minamoto Tamenori's Sanbōe*. Ann Arbor: Center for Japanese Studies, University of Michigan.

Kanda, Christine Guth. 1985. *Shinzō: Hachiman Imagery and Its Development*. Cambridge, Mass.: Council on East Asian Studies, Harvard University.

Kasagidera engi. 1913. *Dainihon bukkyō zensho* 118. Tokyo: Bussho Kankōkai.

Kawachi no kuni Komatsudera engi. 1927. *Zoku Gunshoruijū* 17B. Tokyo: Zoku Gunshoruijū Kanseikai.

Kawakatsu Masatarō. 1971. "Kanjinsō ni kansuru kōsatsu." In *Ōtemae Jōshi Daigaku ronshū* 5.

———. 1972. "Gyakushu shinkō no shiteki kenkyū." In *Ōtemae Jōshi Daigaku ronshū* 6.

———. 1978. *Nihon sekizō bijutsu jiten*. Tokyo: Tōkyōdō.

Keirstead, Thomas. 1992. *The Geography of Power in Medieval Japan*. Princeton: Princeton University Press.

Kitagawa, Joseph. 1969. "Religions of Japan." In *The Great Asian Religions: An Anthology*, ed. Wing-tsit Chan, Isma'il Rāgī al Fārūqī, Joseph M. Kitagawa, and P. T. Raju. New York: Macmillan Publishing Co.

——. 1987. *On Understanding Japanese Religion.* Princeton: Princeton University Press.

Kobayashi Takeshi. 1965. *Shunjōbō Chōgen shiryō shūsei.* Nara Kokuritsu Bunkazai Kenkyūjo shiryō 4. Tokyo: Yoshikawa Kōbunkan.

——. 1971. *Shunjōbō Chōgen no kenkyū.* Yokohoma: Yūrindō.

Kōfukuji bettō shidai. 1917. *Dainihon bukkyō zensho* 124. Tokyo: Bussho Kankōkai.

Koizumi Yoshiaki. 1975. "Nairanki no shakai hendō." In *Iwanami kōza Nihon rekishi* 6: *Chūsei* 2. Tokyo: Iwanami Shoten.

Kujō Kanezane. 1908. *Gyokuyō.* Ed. Yamada Sadayoshi and Yano Tarō. 2 vols. Tokyo: Takatō Chūzō.

Kumamoto ken no chimei. 1985. *Nihon rekishi chimei taikei* 44. Tokyo: Heibonsha.

Kuroda Toshio. 1975. "Chūsei shaji seiryokuron." In *Iwanami kōza Nihon rekishi* 6: *Chūsei* 2. Tokyo: Iwanami Shoten.

——. 1980. *Jisha seiryoku—mō hitotsu no chūsei shakai.* Tokyo: Iwanami Shoten.

Kuroita Katsumi, ed. 1929. *Hyakurenshō. Shintei zōho kokushi taikei* 11. Tokyo: Yoshikawa Kōbunkan.

——. 1943. *Ryō no shūge. Shintei zōho kokushi taikei* 23. Tokyo: Yoshikawa Kōbunkan.

Kwon, Yung-Hee Kim. 1986. "The Emperor's Songs: Go-Shirakawa and *Ryōjin Hishō Kudenshū.*" *Monumenta Nipponica* 41, 3.

Kyōkai. 1984. *Nihon ryōiki.* Ed. Koizumi Osamu. In *Shinchō Nihon koten shūsei.* Tokyo: Shinchōsha.

LaFleur, William R. 1983. *The Karma of Words: Buddhism and the Literary Arts in Medieval Japan.* Berkeley: University of California Press.

Le Goff, Jacques. 1984. *The Birth of Purgatory.* Trans. Arthur Goldhammer. Chicago: University of Chicago Press.

Leyser, Henrietta. 1984. *Hermits and the New Monasticism: A Study of Religious Communities in Western Europe, 1000–1150.* New York: St. Martin's Press.

Little, Lester K. 1978. *Religious Poverty and the Profit Economy in Medieval Europe.* Ithaca: Cornell University Press.

Marra, Michele. 1991. *The Aesthetics of Discontent: Politics and Reclusion in Medieval Japanese Literature.* Honolulu: University of Hawaii Press.

Mass, Jeffrey P. 1974a. "The Emergence of the Kamakura Bakufu." In *Medieval Japan: Essays in Institutional History,* ed. John W. Hall and Jeffrey P. Mass. New Haven: Yale University Press.

——. 1974b. "*Jitō* Land Possession in the Thirteenth Century: The Case of *Shitaji Chūbun.*" In *Medieval Japan: Essays in Institutional*

History, ed. John W. Hall and Jeffrey P. Mass. New Haven: Yale University Press.

———. 1976. *The Kamakura Bakufu: A Study in Documents.* Stanford: Stanford University Press.

Matsunaga, Daigan, and Alicia Matsunaga. 1974–1976. *Foundation of Japanese Buddhism.* 2 vols. Los Angeles: Buddhist Books International.

Matsuo Kenji. 1982. "Kanjin no taiseika to chūsei ritsusō—Kamakura kōki kara nanbokuchōki o chūshin ni shite." *Nihonshi kenkyū* 240.

McCullough, Helen C., trans. 1988. *The Tale of the Heike.* Stanford: Stanford University Press.

McMullin, Neil. 1984. *Buddhism and the State in Sixteenth-Century Japan.* Princeton: Princeton University Press.

———. 1989. "Historical and Historiographical Issues in the Study of Pre-Modern Japanese Religions." *Japanese Journal of Religious Studies* 16, 1.

———. 1992. "Which Doctrine? Whose 'Religion'?—A Rejoinder." *Japanese Journal of Religious Studies* 19, 1.

Minamoto Tamenori. 1982. *Sanbōekotoba.* Ed. Eguchi Takao. 2 vols. Tokyo: Gendai Shichōsha.

Miura Keiichi. 1978. "Kamakura jidai ni okeru kaihotsu to kanjin." *Nihonshi kenkyū* 195.

Mizukami Ichikyū. 1969. *Chūsei no shōen to shakai.* Tokyo: Yoshikawa Kōbunkan.

Mōri Hisashi. 1976. "Shunjōbō Chōgen to busshi Kaikei." *Bukkyō geijutsu* 105.

Mori Katsumi. 1973. "Sōdōsen ryūtsū e no kiban." *Nihon rekishi* 300.

Morrell, Robert E. 1983. "Jōkei and the Kōfukuji Petition." *Japanese Journal of Religious Studies* 10, 1.

———, trans. 1985. *Sand and Pebbles (Shasekishū): The Tales of Mujū Ichien, a Voice for Pluralism in Kamakura Buddhism.* Albany: State University of New York Press.

———. 1987. *Early Kamakura Buddhism: A Minority Report.* Berkeley: Asian Humanities Press.

Mujū Ichien. 1966. *Shasekishū.* Ed. Watanabe Tsunaya. *Nihon koten bungaku taikei* 85. Tokyo: Iwanami Shoten.

Nagahara Keiji. 1968. *Nihon no chūsei shakai.* Tokyo: Iwanami Shoten.

———. 1970. *Nihon keizaishi.* Tokyo: Yūhikaku.

———. 1977. "Village Communities and Daimyo Power." With Kozo Yamamura. In *Japan in the Muromachi Age,* ed. John W. Hall and Toyoda Takeshi. Berkeley: University of California Press.

Nagai Yoshinori. 1953. "Kanjin hijiri to setsuwashū." *Kokugo kokubun* 22:10.

Nagamura Makoto. 1980. "Kamakuraki Tōdaiji kanjinjo no seiritsu to shokatsudō." *Nanto bukkyō* 43–44.

———. 1981. "Tōdaiji daikanjinshiki to 'zenritsusō.' " *Nantō bukkyō* 47.

———. 1989. *Chūsei Tōdaiji no soshiki to keiei.* Tokyo: Hanawa Shobō.

Nagazumi Yasuaki and Ikegami Jun'ichi, eds. 1966–1968. *Konjaku monogatarishū, honchōbu.* 6 vols. Tokyo: Heibonsha.

Nakamura Kyoko, trans. 1973. *Miraculous Stories from the Japanese Buddhist Tradition: The Nihon Ryōiki of the Monk Kyōkai.* Cambridge, Mass.: Harvard University Press.

Nakanodō Isshin. 1970. "Chūseiteki kanjin no keisei katei." In *Chūsei no kenryoku to minshū*, ed. Nihonshi Kenkyūkai Shiryō Kenkyūbukai. Osaka: Sōgensha.

———. 1975. "Tōdaiji daikanjinshiki no seiritsu—'Shunjōbō Chōgen' zō no zaikentō." *Nihonshi kenkyū* 152.

———. 1978. "Chūseiteki kanjin no tenkai." *Geinōshi kenkyū* 62.

Nakao Takashi. 1977. "Chōgen o chūshin to suru kanjin hijiri shūdan no soshikika to teichaku—Tōdaiji shōryō dōsha bessho no keisei to un'ei o megutte." *Shūkyō shakaishi kenkyū*, ed. Risshō Daigaku Shigakkai. Tokyo: Yūzankaku.

Nara Kokuritsu Bunkazai Kenkyūjo. 1977. *Saidaiji Eizon denki shūsei.* Tokyo: Hōzōkan.

Nara Kokuritsu Hakubutsukan. 1973. *(Shinkan rakusei kinen) Kyōzuka ihōten.* Nara: Nara National Museum.

Ohnuki-Tierney, Emiko. 1987. *The Monkey as Mirror: Symbolic Transformations in Japanese History and Ritual.* Princeton: Princeton University Press.

Okayama ken no chimei. 1988. *Nihon rekishi chimei taikei* 34. Tokyo: Heibonsha.

Panofsky, Erwin. 1979. *Abbot Suger on the Abbey Church of St.-Denis and Its Art Treasures.* (Second edition prepared by Gerda Panofsky-Soergel.) Princeton: Princeton University Press.

Piggott, Joan R. 1982. "Hierarchy and Economics in Early Medieval Tōdaiji." In *Court and Bakufu in Japan: Essays in Kamakura History*, ed. Jeffrey P. Mass. New Haven: Yale University Press.

———. 1987. "Tōdaiji and the Nara Imperium." Ph.D. dissertation, Stanford University.

Ruch, Barbara. 1977. "Medieval Jongleurs and the Making of a National Literature." In *Japan in the Muromachi Age*, ed. John W. Hall and Toyoda Takeshi. Berkeley: University of California Press.

———. 1990. "The Other Side of Culture in Medieval Japan." In *The Cambridge History of Japan* 3: *Medieval Japan*, ed. Kozo Yamamura. Cambridge, England, and New York: Cambridge University Press.

Sakurai Tokutarō, Hagiwara Tatsuo, and Miyata Noboru. 1975. *Jisha engi. Nihon shisō taikei* 20. Tokyo: Iwanami Shoten.

Sansom, George B. 1958. *A History of Japan to 1334.* Stanford: Stanford University Press.

Sasaki Kōshō. 1987. *Bukkyō minzokushi no kenkyū.* Tokyo: Meicho Shuppan.

Sawa Takaaki. 1972. *Art in Japanese Esoteric Buddhism.* Trans. Richard L. Gage. *The Heibonsha Survey of Japanese Art* 8. New York and Tokyo: John Weatherhill/Heibonsha.

Sei Shōnagon. 1977. *Makura no sōshi* (Pillow Book). Ed. Hagitani Boku. 2 vols. Tokyo: Shinchōsha.

Shimizu Shunmyō. 1973. *Yamato no sekibutsu.* Osaka: Sōgensha.

Solomon, Ira M. 1972. "Rennyo and the Rise of Honganji in Muromachi Japan." Ph.D. dissertation, Columbia University.

Sōshō. 1960. *Miroku nyorai kannōshō.* In *Tōdaiji Sōshō shōnin no kenkyū narabi ni shiryō* 3, ed. Hiraoka Jōkai. Tokyo: Nihon Gakujutsu Shinkōkai.

Sponberg, Alan, and Helen Hardacre. 1988. *Maitreya, the Future Buddha.* Cambridge, England, and New York: Cambridge University Press.

Taira Masayuki. 1984. "Chūsei shūkyō no shakaiteki tenkai." In *(Kōza) Nihon rekishi* 3: *Chūsei* 1, ed. Rekishigaku Kenkyūkai and Nihonshi Kenkyūkai. Tokyo University.

Takakusu Junjirō and Watanabe Kaigyoku, eds. 1924–1932. *Taishō shinshu daizōkyō.* 100 vols. Tokyo: Taishō Issaikyō Kankōkai.

Takeuchi Rizō. 1963–1976. *Heian ibun.* 13 vols. Tokyo: Tōkyōdō.

———. 1971–1991. *Kamakura ibun.* 42 vols. plus indexes. Tokyo: Tōkyōdō.

———. 1978. *Kodai kara chūsei e.* Tokyo: Yoshikawa Kōbunkan.

Takizawa Takeo. 1970. "Heian kōki no kahei ni tsuite." *Shikan* 82.

Tanabe, George J., Jr., and Willa Jane Tanabe, eds. 1989. *The Lotus Sutra in Japanese Culture.* Honolulu: University of Hawaii Press.

Tanaka Fumihide. 1984. "Chūsei zenki no jiin to minshū." *Nihonshi kenkyū* 266.

Tanaka Tan. 1976. "Chōgen no zōei katsudō." *Bukkyō geijutsu* 105.

Teiser, Stephen F. 1988. *The Ghost Festival in Medieval China.* Princeton: Princeton University Press.

Tōdaiji yōroku. 1907. *Zokuzoku gunshoruijū* 11. Tokyo: Kokusho Kankōkai.

Tōdaiji zoku yōroku. 1907. *Zokuzoku gunshoruijū* 11. Tokyo: Kokusho Kankōkai.

Tomimura Takafumi. 1977. "Jōkei no dōyū to deshitachi." In *Shūkyō shakaishi kenkyū,* ed. Risshō Daigaku Shigakkai. Tokyo: Yūzankaku.

Tsunoda Ryusaku, William Theodore de Bary, and Donald Keene. 1958. *Sources of Japanese Tradition.* New York: Columbia University Press.

Tsuruoka Shizuo. 1967. "Kamakura jidai no itabi ni arawareta shinkō keitai." In *(Hōken kindai ni okeru) Kamakura bukkyō no tenkai,* ed. Kasahara Kazuo. Tokyo: Hōzōkan.

Turner, Victor. 1969. *The Ritual Process: Structure and Anti-Structure.* Chicago: Aldine Publishing Co.

————. 1974. *Dramas, Fields, and Metaphors: Symbolic Action in Human Society.* Ithaca: Cornell University Press.

Tyler, Royall. 1990. *The Miracles of the Kasuga Deity.* New York: Columbia University Press.

Tyler, Susan C. 1992. *The Cult of Kasuga as Seen Through Its Art.* Ann Arbor: Center for Japanese Studies, University of Michigan.

Ueda Sachiko. 1976. "Eizon to Yamato no Saidaiji matsuji." In *Chūsei shakai no seiritsu to tenkai,* ed. Ōsaka Rekishi Gakkai. Tokyo: Yoshikawa Kōbunkan.

Ury, Marian. 1979. *Tales of Times Now Past: Sixty-two Stories from a Medieval Japanese Collection.* Berkeley: University of California Press.

Wajima Yoshio. 1959. *Eizon, Ninshō.* Tokyo: Yoshikawa Kōbunkan.

Wakita Haruko. 1975. "Towards a Wider Perspective on Medieval Commerce." *Journal of Japanese Studies* 1:2.

Washio Junkei. 1966. *Nihon bukke jinmei jisho.* Orig. pub. 1902–1903. Tokyo: Tōkyō Bijutsu.

Wata Shūjō. 1976. "Kōyasan to Chōgen oyobi Kan'amidabutsu." *Bukkyō geijutsu* 105.

Watson, James L. 1988. "Funeral Specialists in Cantonese Society: Pollution, Performance, and Social Hierarchy." In *Death Ritual in Late Imperial and Modern China,* ed. James L. Watson and Evelyn Rawski. Berkeley: University of California Press.

Yashima Kyōsuke. 1959. "Honpō ni okeru shutsudo senka." *Nihon kōkōgaku kōza 7: rekishi jidai (chūsei, kinsei).* Tokyo: Kawade Shobō.

Yamaguchi Masao. 1977. "Kingship, Theatricality, and Marginal Reality in Japan." In *Text and Context: The Social Anthropology of Tradition,* ed. Ravindra Jain. Philadelphia: Institute for the Study of Human Issues.

Yasuda Tsuguo. 1983. "Kanjin no taiseika to 'hyakushō'—Yamato no hitokoku heikinyaku = dochōyaku ni tsuite." *Shigaku zasshi* 92:1.

Yoshida Fumio. 1972. "Nanto bukkyō no fukkō." *Ajia bukkyōshi Nihon hen 5: Kamakura bukkyō 3,* ed. Nakamura Hajime, Kasahara Kazuo, and Kanaoka Shūyū. Tokyo: Kōsei Shuppansha.

Index

About the Author

Janet R. Goodwin, since receiving her doctorate from the University of California, Berkeley, has taught Japanese history and civilization at several California universities, most recently at the University of California, Los Angeles, and the University of Southern California. Her research, which has focused on the cultural, social, and religious history of medieval Japan, has been published in *Journal of Asian Studies, Monumenta Nipponica,* and *Japanese Journal of Religious Studies.* In 1993 she assumed the position of professor of cultural studies at the University of Aizu in Aizu-Wakamatsu City, Japan.

Production Notes

Composition and paging were done on the
Quadex Composing System and typesetting
on the Compugraphic 8400 by the design
and production staff of University of
Hawaii Press.

The text and display typeface is Baskerville.

Offset presswork and binding were done by
The Maple-Vail Book Manufacturing Group.
Text paper is Glatfelter Offset Vellum,
basis 50.